English

Ausgabe G · Große Ausgabe

Band 6 A
für das 10. Schuljahr
an Gymnasien
und Gesamtschulen

Cornelsen & Oxford University Press

ENGLISH · Ausgabe G
Band 6 A für das 10. Schuljahr an Gymnasien und Gesamtschulen

Erarbeitet von
Cornelsen-Velhagen & Klasing Verlag für Lehrmedien, Berlin

Verlagsredaktion
Martin Rosenthal, Michael Ferguson und David W. Bygott

in Zusammenarbeit mit
Cornelsen & Oxford University Press, Berlin,

und den nachstehenden Mitarbeitern
Prof. Hellmut Schwarz, Mannheim · Prof. Franz Vettel, Heppenheim ·
Prof. Dieter Vater, Weinheim · OSchR Burkhart Nather, Mülheim (Ruhr)
sowie John Eastwood, Ilkley · Dr. Volker Saftien, Lörrach (Entwurf der
Communication practice Exercises)

Beratende Mitwirkung
RR Rudolf Bäulke, Moringen · OStD Dr. Klaus Becker, Wilhelmshaven ·
RR Herbert Brosowsky, Varel · OSchR Edgar Dietz, Weil am Rhein ·
StD Erich Fleischhack, Ebern/Unterfranken · StD Roland Grimm, Mudau/Odenwald ·
RL Hans-H. Meißner, Moringen · StD Bernd Sülzer, Köln

Zeichnungen
Robert Broomfield, Tunbridge Wells

1. Auflage – 8. Druck 1984
Bestellnummer 70549

© Cornelsen-Velhagen & Klasing GmbH & Co.
 Verlag für Lehrmedien KG, Berlin, 1978

Alle Rechte vorbehalten.
Die Vervielfältigung und Übertragung, auch einzelner Textabschnitte, Bilder oder Zeichnungen, ist – mit Ausnahme der Vervielfältigung zum persönlichen und eigenen Gebrauch gemäß §§ 53, 54 URG – ohne schriftliche Zustimmung des Verlages nicht zulässig.
Das gilt sowohl für die Vervielfältigung durch Fotokopie oder irgendein anderes Verfahren als auch für die Übertragung auf Filme, Bänder, Platten, Arbeitstransparente oder andere Medien.

Druck: CVK-Druck, Berlin

ISBN 3-464-07054-9

Vertrieb: Cornelsen-Velhagen & Klasing Verlagsgesellschaft, Bielefeld

Contents

Unit	Page	Parts of the unit	Teaching items
1	6	**A**cquisition: Politics in Britain	The passive: The school is said/thought/believed to be excellent. – His arm got broken in the accident. – I want/would like this jacket cleaned. – -ing form (gerund) in passive · More about modals and auxiliaries: I may be late. Tom said he might be late. – When are we to be back? – (The Queen is to visit France. – I shall read the book first. We should appreciate an early reply. – Jill will/would often play for hours.) · REVISION – Modals: some ways of expressing obligation
	10	Text **Two MPs talk to ENGLISH G**	
	14	**Ex**ercises	
	24	Communication practice: Reproaching people and reacting to reproaches	
	26	**S**ummary	
2	30	Acquisition: The English language	Phrasal verbs: put away/on/up/through, turn down/on/off/over/round, etc. · I turned the light out./I turned out the light./I turned it out. · More about present participles: He introduced himself, shaking hands with everyone. – They left the room talking excitedly. – Jane sat in the living-room watching TV. – He came running into the room. · Word order: inversion after *never, hardly, no sooner,* etc. · (Here comes the bus.) · If-clauses with *should*: We'll let you know if we should change our plans. · Omission of *if* + inversion: Should we change our plans, we'll let you know. · (will/would in the if-clause) · REVISION – Sentences with if-clauses
	34	*T 1 **Where does English come from?**	
	36	T 2 **It's nice, isn't it?**	
	37	T 3 **There was a young ...**	
	38	Exercises	
	46	Communication practice: Hesitating	
	47	Summary	

*wahlfrei

Unit	Page	Parts of the unit	Teaching items
3	50	Acquisition: Energy problems	REVISION – Reported speech · (More about reported speech: no tense
	57	T **Oil man**	change with introducing verb in present/ present perfect/future · no tense change when statement is still true · no change of simple past/past progressive · change or no change with *must/needn't/ mustn't*) · More about possessives: Their action saved our lives. – a friend of mine, of hers, etc. – a room of my own. · Concord with *somebody/nobody/everybody*: Everybody sends their love.
	63	Exercises	
	70	Communication practice: Making requests and responding to them	
	72	Summary	
4	76	A/T **Learning to appreciate literature: some poems and narrative texts**	REVISION – Simple and progressive aspects in different tenses
	99	Exercises	
	106	Communication practice: Avoiding bluntness	
	107	Summary	

	110	Translation practice
	116	Using a dictionary (Hinweise zur Benutzung eines englisch-deutschen Wörterbuches)
	118	Notes on the authors in Unit 4
	119	Names
	120	Irregular verbs
	122	Phrasal verbs
	123	English words and phrases
	148	List of words
	153	Deutsch-englische Übersetzungsstücke

Das auf Seite 31 genannte Project Book hat folgende Bestellnummer:
Project Book 3: A COMMON LANGUAGE, Best.-Nr. 5054

Zu diesem Lehrbuch ist eine Compact-Cassette erschienen. Sie enthält wortgetreue Wiedergaben fast aller Texte, Dialoge und Gedichte, sowie Auszüge aus 2 A und 2 CP. Bestellung beim Verlag oder in jeder Buchhandlung.
CVK-Bestellnummer 8428.

Bildquellen: Bavaria-Verlag, Gauting, S. 50 (oben), 55 (unten rechts – W. Pabst); BP, London, S. 54, 60, 61; Ron Burton, Grimsby, S. 7 (rechts); Camera Press Ltd., London, S. 8; Cornelsen-Velhagen & Klasing, Berlin, S. 13 (links), 35 und 97 (P. W. Oldham); Deutsche Presse-Agentur, Frankfurt a. Main, S. 55 (oben links und rechts); Esso A.G., Hamburg, S. 59; Ewing Galloway, New York, S. 50 (unten); Grimsby Evening Telegraph, Grimsby, S. 9; The Labour Party, Nottingham, S. 7 (links); Monkmeyer Press Photo Service, New York, S. 51 (unten rechts); The News, Portsmouth, S. 12 (links); Popperfoto, London, S. 6; Punch Publications Ltd., London, S. 13 (rechts); Sheffield Newspapers Ltd., Sheffield, S. 12 (rechts); Dennis Skinner, Bolsover, S. 10 (rechts); Universal Pictorial Press & Agency Ltd., London, S. 10 (links); United Features Syndicate, S. 56; United States Embassy, S. 55 (unten links).
Einband: K. Wagener (Cornelsen-Velhagen & Klasing, Berlin).

Textquellen: Statistical information p. 8 taken from THE TIMES GUIDE TO THE HOUSE OF COMMONS OCTOBER 1974, © 1974 by Times Newspapers Ltd.
Statistical information in table p. 30 taken from THE WORLD ALMANAC & BOOK OF FACTS 1978, © 1977 by Newspaper Enterprise Association, Inc.
Statistical information p. 32 taken from BRITAIN 1978, AN OFFICIAL HANDBOOK, H.M.S.O., © 1978 Crown copyright.
Cockney shop assistant quotation p. 33 from ADOLESCENT BOYS IN EAST LONDON by P. Willmott, © 1966 by Institute of Community Studies.
It's nice, isn't it? by George Mikes reprinted by permission from HOW TO BE AN ALIEN, © by André Deutsch.
Stopping by woods on a snowy evening by Robert Frost reprinted by permission from THE POETRY OF ROBERT FROST, © Holt, Rinehart & Winston.
The Icingbus by Roger McGough reprinted by permission from PENGUIN MODERN POETS 10, © 1967 by Roger McGough.
Pantomime Poem by Roger McGough reprinted by permission from AFTER THE MERRYMAKING published by Jonathan Cape Ltd.
loneliness reprinted by permission from COMPLETE POEMS by E. E. Cummings published by MacGibbon & Kee Ltd./Granada Publishing Ltd.
Tonight at noon by Adrian Henri reprinted by permission of Deborah Rogers Ltd., London, from THE MERSEY SOUND (Penguin Modern Poets 10), © 1967 by Adrian Henri.
Leisure by W. H. Davies reprinted by permission of Mrs H. M. Davies from THE COMPLETE POEMS OF W. H. DAVIES published by Jonathan Cape Ltd.
Viewing Time by E. V. Milner reprinted by permission of Punch Publications Ltd., London.
The Little Girl and the Wolf, The Peacelike Mongoose and *The Rabbits who caused All the Trouble* (+ illustrations) reprinted by permission from THE THURBER CARNIVAL, the Collection Copyright © 1963 by James Thurber.
Do You Like It Here? reprinted by permission of Random House, Inc., from THE O'HARA GENERATION by John O'Hara, © 1939 and renewed 1967 by John O'Hara; originally appeared in THE NEW YORKER.
And Miles to go before I Sleep by W. F. Nolan, reprinted from IMPACT – 20: EXCURSIONS INTO THE EXTRAORDINARY, © 1963 by Paperback Literary Inc.
Little Johnny's Confession by Brian Patten reprinted by permission of George Allen & Unwin Ltd.
I Can Tell Wops a Mile Off reprinted by permission of Charles Scribner's Sons from IN OUR TIME by Ernest Hemingway, © 1925 by Charles Scribner's Sons.
Dictionary quotation pp. 116/117 from LANGENSCHEIDTS HANDWÖRTERBUCH ENGLISCH, Teil I, © 1964, 1967 Langenscheidt KG.

Unit 1 A

1. Who has the political power in Britain? Who decides whether more nuclear power stations are needed or where they'll be built, and how much of the taxpayer's money should be spent on defence, pensions or schools? Who makes important decisions like these which affect the whole nation? Is it the Queen?

2. Well, officially the Queen is the head of the country[1], but she has no power to make political decisions. Each year, for example, when she visits the Houses of Parliament[2] to read the Queen's Speech, everyone knows she didn't write it herself.

   Some nurses giving a petition to Mr William Benyon, MP

   The programme she describes is in fact prepared by the Government – the Prime Minister and the other ministers in his Cabinet[3] – who, of course, take advice from their top civil servants. Moreover, this programme can only be turned into laws if a majority of the politicians in the House of Commons agree. So the final responsibility lies with the 635 Members of Parliament (MPs).

3. Every MP is elected to the Commons individually by the voters in one area of Britain, and he (or she) then represents this area at Westminster. The 635 separate areas, called constituencies, are each supposed to have about 60,000 voters, but that's only an average of course.
   Let's see how a new MP was elected in one such constituency[4].

Some background notes

[1] In contrast to the Federal Republic of Germany, the U.K. is a monarchy.
[2] Parliament consists of two Houses: the House of Commons and the House of Lords. The members of the Commons are elected by the country's voters; the roughly 1100 members of the Lords have either inherited their title or been appointed. Both the Commons and the Lords discuss bills, but the Commons has the final word. A bill turned down by the Lords will still become law if a majority in the Commons insists on it.
[3] The Prime Minister is the leader of the largest party in the Commons. The leader of the second largest becomes the Leader of the Opposition.
[4] At least once every five years a general election is held: each of the 635 constituencies elects an MP on the same day. An extra election, or by-election, might be necessary in a particular constituency, e.g. if the MP there dies.

4 In February 1977 Anthony Crosland, Britain's Foreign Secretary and MP for the fishing port of Grimsby, died suddenly. So it was announced that a by-election would be held on Thursday, 28th April to elect a new MP. There were 6 candidates altogether, but only 2 **were thought to** have a chance of winning: Labour's new man and the Conservative, the candidate of the other big party. The other 4 candidates **weren't expected to** be "in the race". Who would win?

The results in Grimsby at the general election on 10.10.74	
Candidates	Votes
Crosland (LABOUR)	21,657 (47.1%)
Brown (CONSERVATIVE)	14,675 (31.9%)
Rigby (LIBERAL)	9,487 (20.6%)
McElrea (IND DEM LAB)	166 (0.4%)
Result for the Labour Party: 1 MP	
Result for the other parties: –	

S 1a · Ex 2a, b

5

Labour

Austin Mitchell, aged 42
TV interviewer. Not a local man, but well-known from TV news programmes.
He says:
He will fight to protect the local fishing industry. The Common Market has given Britain higher food prices, but Labour has stopped them from going up faster and has reduced taxes. Working people should vote Labour. The Tories would give more profits to the rich.

VOTE **AUSTIN MITCHELL** LABOUR X
VOTE LABOUR
Thursday **28** APRIL

Liberal

Andrew De Freitas, aged 32
Official in the fishing industry. On the town council since 1970.
He says:
More help for the local fishing industry. More power to local councils. People are fed up with 2 big parties – one that represents big business, and one that represents the unions. Everyone's vote should count.

Stop!
Think!
GO Liberal!

SOCIALIST WORKERS PARTY
Michael Stanton, aged 24
Docker. Wants workers to have more power. No hope of winning. Hopes to gain 25 new members for his party.

SUNSHINE PARTY
Peter Bishop, aged 47
Retired scientist. Only member of this party. Policies totally unclear.

MALCOLM MUGGERIDGE FAN CLUB
Max Nottingham, aged 50
Unemployed clerk. Only member of this party. Policies unclear. The press called him "the second most idiotic candidate" of the campaign.

Conservative

Robbie Blair, aged 51
Fish buyer for frozen food factories. Married to a trawler captain's daughter.
He says:
Reduce public spending, Control prices better. Spend more on defence. Unions shouldn't try to run the country: that's Parliament's job. The Labour government hasn't protected the fishing industry properly. Stricter punishment for crime. More discipline in schools.

YOU KNOW THE PRICE OF SOCIALISM…
● TAXES UP
● PRICES UP
● JOBS DOWN
For GRIMSBY'S SAKE VOTE
BLAIR
CONSERVATIVE

1 A

6 The <u>party agents</u> prepared <u>leaflets</u> <u>explaining</u> their candidate's <u>views on</u> the <u>key issues</u>. The candidates themselves <u>gave press conferences</u> and were <u>interviewed on TV</u>. They had <u>to be willing to work</u> long hours: speaking at <u>meetings, shaking hands with shoppers</u>, and <u>knocking on front doors</u> to talk to people. **Being recognized** and <u>remembered</u> was their <u>main target</u>. They **wanted** their names **to be repeated** <u>as often as possible</u> and **wanted** their views **reported** in all the papers.

S 1c, d · Ex 4, 5, 6

7 One <u>keen</u> young <u>party helper</u> who <u>canvassed for</u> the Conservatives was 17-year-old Carol Ross, a <u>sixth former</u> at the same school as Robbie Blair's daughter Felicity. Carol <u>delivered</u> leaflets after school, gave her friends <u>stickers</u> <u>to wear</u> and helped in the party agent's office <u>at weekends</u>. Thanks to Carol, a lot of VOTE BLAIR posters **got put up** in people's windows and <u>at school</u> – though she herself wasn't allowed to put one up at home, as her parents <u>supported</u> the Liberals!

S 1b · Ex 3

<u>Hard at work</u> in the party agent's office

More <u>notes on</u> British elections

1. Voters <u>must be aged at least 18</u>. Each voter has one vote.
2. <u>The winning candidate</u> is the one who gets most votes, a <u>simple majority</u> of one vote being enough.
3. The results of the general election on 10.10.1974:

	Total votes	Seats
Labour	11,468,136 (39.3%)	319 (50.2%)
Conservative	10,464,675 (35.8%)	277 (43.6%)
Liberal	5,346,800 (18.3%)	13 (2.1%)
Others	1,908,995 (6.6%)	26 (4.1%)

- The Liberal candidate in Grimsby, Andrew De Freitas, thinks everyone's vote should count (see page 7). He would prefer a system <u>based on</u> <u>Proportional Representation</u>. Look at the October 1974 results and say why. Try to find a few differences between the British and German <u>election systems</u>.

1 A

8   Carol's boy-friend, Frank, an apprentice at a chemical factory, happened to hear Austin Mitchell speak outside the factory gate at 7.30 one morning. Afterwards Frank asked his friends whether they were going to vote for him. Pat Darley, a union official, said: "Of course." Len Beckett wasn't so sure: "Perhaps I will. Or I **may** vote Tory. I was told Blair might bring more jobs to the area. That's what we need, isn't it?" Sandra Holmes, a wages clerk, said: "Hmm. They're all the same. We**'re to** wait another year for more pay, that's what they tell us. But meanwhile prices keep going up every week – and we're to put up with that. Well, I'm not going to vote at all. It's not worth it."

S 2a, b, (c) · Ex 7, 8

9   Grimsby had been a "safe" Labour seat since 1945. However, the opinion polls said the Labour Party was likely to lose this time. Suddenly, the government announced a special development programme for Grimsby. This meant that more public money would be invested there, the port's links with the national motorway network would be improved and unemployment reduced. Of course, everyone was delighted. At the same time the government was accused of trying to make the Labour candidate popular. "How can you announce something of such importance just before a by-election?" their opponents demanded to be told. "We **shall** not accept this! It's bribery! Manipulation!"

S 2 (d), (e)

10 After school on polling day Carol Ross set off in Frank's old car to give a lift to some Conservative voters who might otherwise have stayed at home. Then, at 10 pm, the polling stations were no sooner closed than the votes began to be counted. According to the opinion polls Robbie Blair was still the clear favourite, but it was soon neck and neck between him and Austin Mitchell. In fact, it was so close that they were obliged to recount the votes twice. The winner wasn't finally announced until the early hours of the Friday morning. The Labour supporters cheered. The man who would take his seat in the House of Commons the following Tuesday as Grimsby's new MP was Austin Mitchell!
Here are the full results:

A. Mitchell (LAB)	21,890	(46.9%)
R. Blair (CON)	21,370	(45.8%)
A. De Freitas (LIB)	3,128	(6.7%)
M. Stanton (SWP)	215	(0.4%)
P. Bishop (SUNSHINE)	64	(0.1%)
M. Nottingham (MMFC)	30	(0.06%)
Majority: 520 votes		

● *What methods are used to win votes? Which do you think are most effective? Why?*

1 T

Two MPs talk to ENGLISH G

In order to obtain an up-to-date picture of a Member of Parliament, ENGLISH G asked 17 MPs to talk about themselves, their views and their jobs. Five MPs gave very detailed replies. They included Anthony Nelson, MP for Chichester, and Dennis Skinner, MP for Bolsover.

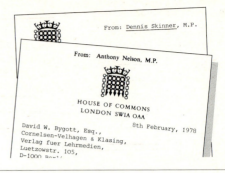

ANTHONY NELSON (Conservative)
Born: 11.6.1948 (in Hamburg)
Education: Public school and Cambridge University **Career:** Was a banker in the City of London. **Hobbies:** Music, rugby, travelling **Election record:** A losing candidate in Leeds[1] at the general election in Feb 1974. Elected in Chichester (a city in the south of England, 65 miles from London) in Oct 1974. **In constituency:** Every weekend, plus a lot of evenings. Arranges special times every fortnight, when his constituents can talk to him about their problems, views, etc.

DENNIS SKINNER (Labour)
Born: 11.2.1932 **Education:** Grammar school and Ruskin College[2]
Career: A coal-miner for 21 years. A town councillor. Became president of his trade union in 1966. **Hobbies:** Athletics, walking, cycling, tennis
Election record: Elected in Bolsover (a town in the Midlands, 150 miles from London) in 1970. Re-elected in Feb 1974 and Oct 1974.
In constituency: Nearly all the time when the Commons is "on holiday". (Otherwise shares a flat in London with another Labour MP, and only sees his family at weekends.) His constituents can see him every weekend.

Two men doing the same job but with very different backgrounds. Are their views just as different? Let them speak for themselves. Here are some of the things they said.

ENGLISH G: Why did you become an MP?

A. N.: I became interested in politics when 21, partly through my interest in penal reform. I was elected at the age of 26.
D. S.: I was asked to be a candidate in Bolsover by my trade union. Unlike many other MPs, I did not search the U.K. for a suitable constituency.

EG: What were your feelings on entering the Commons as a new MP?

A. N.: I felt very excited and proud. I feel the same now.
D. S.: To me Parliament was my new workplace – no more, no less. I cannot remember having any feelings of excitement, etc. Similarly, I cannot remember anything special about my first day going to work in a coal-mine. I simply had a good look round and studied the working conditions.

Editor's notes:
[1] In the north of England, 190 miles from London, 6th biggest city in the U.K.
[2] A college where adult workers are sponsored by their trade unions.

EG: Is it an MP's duty to represent the views of his constituents, his party, his trade union, or any other group?

    A.N.: An MP has a responsibility to his constituents. But he must be able to vote according to his conscience and his own judgement.
    D.S.: No man living, either in Parliament or outside, can represent conflicting interests. Therefore, I cannot represent the bankers and the workers at the same time. I at all times represent my class.

EG: Can you describe a case where you, or a fellow MP, found it difficult to decide who to support when voting on a matter in the Commons?[3]

    A.N.: No.
    D.S.: There are too many to mention.

EG: In whose hands is the real power to make policies and laws today?

	A.N.	D.S.
	(marks out of ten)	
a) the voters	6	2
b) the backbenchers	6	3
c) the 635 MPs	8	4
d) the PM and the Cabinet	9	7
e) the civil servants	5	9
f) the City (bankers, etc.)	1	8
g) multi-national companies	0	7
h) trade unions	5	2
i) somewhere else?	3 (pressure groups)	9 (judges, army, police, Common Market)

EG: How many hours do you spend on different activities in a typical week in the Commons?[4]

	D.S.	A.C.	C.S.
a) Listening to or speaking in debates	12	10	3
b) Attending committee meetings	10	18	3
c) Talking to fellow MPs informally or discussing party policy	10	1	3
d) Research (in the library, etc.)	10	2	0
e) Working at desk in own room	15	6	26
f) Speaking or writing to journalists	$\frac{1}{4}$	$\frac{1}{2}$	2
g) Correspondence with constituents	7	20	21
h) Meeting and acting as a guide to visitors (from constituency, etc.)	2	1	1

[3] Neil Kinnock, Labour MP for Bedwellty, gave ENGLISH G an example. Though he disagreed with the Government's plans to give separate parliaments to Scotland and Wales, he said he would have to vote for them. The plans weren't very good, but voting with the Opposition against a weak Labour Government would be worse.

[4] Anthony Nelson said his answers here would be very different from week to week, so it isn't possible to give the average times for him. The figures given are for Dennis Skinner, Albert Costain (Conservative MP for Folkestone and Hythe) and Cyril Smith (Liberal MP for Rochdale).

1 T

EG: Should MPs have a job outside Parliament?

A. N.: An MP's work makes it difficult to do an outside job, but I think it is valuable and a good discipline for the individual. Is it a good thing that a man can be an MP for, say, 35 years without having experience of any outside job during that time?

D. S.: I am disappointed that so many MPs "line their pockets" with outside jobs. I strongly believe that an MP should give all his/her time and attention to the job for which the taxpayer pays him. I have no doubt that hundreds of MPs must face a conflict of interests because of their outside work.

EG: How much should MPs earn?

A. N.: MPs' salaries are totally inadequate. In order to attract people of suitable quality and ability, the salary should compare with that of, say, a company director or a top civil servant.⁵

D. S.: MPs are quite well paid as compared with, say, a miner. There are plenty of applicants for Parliament, so it must be an attractive job!

EG: What gives you most satisfaction as an MP?

A. N.: Most satisfaction has come from individual cases where I have been able to influence decisions and help constituents. Opportunities to travel and learn about situations in other countries (e.g. Rhodesia and Japan this year) are particularly interesting.

D. S.: I get most satisfaction when I succeed in a case for one of my working-class voters against the bureaucracy.

Receiving a petition about road accidents

Helping a constituent with a rent problem

[5] In 1977 an MP's salary was £6062 p.a. (roughly DM 2000 per month). The Leader of the Opposition got £9500, Cabinet Ministers £16,000 and the Prime Minister £20,000. Top civil servants received £18,675-20,175. Company directors got £7,424-17,430 and in some cases very much more. With overtime payments, miners working underground earned an average of £62.65-87.22 per week.

1 T

1. Mr Nelson became an MP at 26. Do you think this is too early? Why? And what about retiring? Should MPs be obliged to retire at a certain age like, say, airline pilots?
2. According to Mr Skinner, a lot of MPs search the U.K. to find a suitable constituency. What does he mean by "suitable"? What's the key characteristic of a safe seat?
3. Describe the different reactions of the two MPs on entering Parliament.
4. When asked whose views an MP should represent, the two MPs partly agreed. What's the same/different in their answers? What's your opinion?
5. Which Labour MP said he would vote with his party, in spite of disagreeing with one of its policies? What arguments speak for/against doing this?
6. Who has got a lot of/not much political power, according to Mr Nelson and Mr Skinner? Where do the two MPs agree/disagree?
7. Compare the way the three MPs spend their time in the Commons. What would you expect MPs to spend more/less time on? Why?
8. What do Mr Nelson and Mr Skinner see as the advantages/disadvantages of an outside job for MPs? In what circumstances do you think an MP might face a conflict of interests if, for example, he was (a) the director of a cigarette factory, or (b) a trade union official?
9. Mr Nelson and Mr Skinner disagree about MPs' salaries. What are their arguments? How much do you think an MP should earn compared with, say, a miner, shop assistant, fireman, doctor? Why?
10. What gives the two MPs most satisfaction about being an MP? Do they agree or is there a difference? What would you like and dislike most, if you were an MP?

"…and if you re-elect me to be your Member of Parliament, ladies and gentlemen, I promise to keep all those promises I made five years ago."

"The Queen was delighted with the draft for her speech, er, except for one or two places where she added a comma."

1 The passive

 opening a polling station

 giving a ballot paper to a voter

 putting a cross on the paper

 folding the paper and putting it in the ballot box

 closing the polling station

 taking the ballot boxes to the local town hall

 counting the votes

 declaring the result

a *Say what is happening in these pictures.*

1. A polling station is being opened.
2. A voter ... a ballot paper.   *Go on.*

b *Imagine you're a journalist from India on a visit to Britain. Describe for your magazine what you saw on election day. Try and mention things that aren't in the pictures, too. Begin like this:*

Election day was, as always, on a Thursday. The polling stations were opened at 7 o'clock. Each voter who arrived at the polling station ... a ballot paper with the candidates' names on it. After a cross ... on the paper next to one of the names, the paper ... and ... in a ballot box. During the day hundreds of people ...   *Go on.*

*c *Now write a paragraph saying what happens on election day in West Germany. Begin like this:*

In West Germany election day is always on a ....

Rev.

2 a *Some MPs are talking to a reporter about the government's difficulties. But they don't want the reporter to mention their names in his newspaper.*

1. I believe the PM has had an argument with several Cabinet members...
2. I've heard reports that the Cabinet is divided over economic policy...
3. I expect MPs will turn down the government's new tax plan...
4. I think support for the PM has almost disappeared...
5. Everyone supposes the Minister for Europe is thinking of retiring from politics...
6. We all know two leading ministers are in trouble about their income tax...
7. They say the Minister of Education is fed up with her job...
8. MPs consider that the Minister of Employment has failed at his job...

How was this information reported the next day in the newspaper?

1. The Prime Minister is believed to have had an argument ... .
2. The Cabinet is reported to be ... .
3. MPs are expected ... .   Go on.

b *Over the following days and weeks, the statements had to be brought up to date. Use the same passive pattern in the sentences, but be careful with the tense of the verbs.*

1. last week/PM/believe/have had an argument with several Cabinet members,/he/report/have made peace with them meanwhile
   Although last week the Prime Minister was believed to have had an argument with several Cabinet members, he is reported to have made peace with them meanwhile.
2. some days ago/Cabinet/report/be divided over economic policy,/they/think/be united again now
   Although some days ago the Cabinet was reported to be divided ... .
3. according to earlier reports/MPs/expect/turn down the government's new tax plan,/the majority/consider/be in favour of it now
4. quite recently/support for the PM/think/have almost disappeared,/much of it/believe/be returning this week
5. last month/Minister for Europe/suppose/be thinking of retiring,/he/say/think differently about it now
6. at the weekend/two leading ministers/know/be in trouble about their income tax,/they/suppose/have denied it meanwhile
7. not long ago/Minister of Education/say/be fed up with her job,/she now/know/be interested in continuing
8. according to earlier reports/Minister of Employment/consider/have failed at his job,/he now/expect/be given even greater powers

3 Here are some notes made by a policeman at an accident between two cars.

```
Mini 1000 passengers :-
Mr Don Elliott — knee hurt, couldn't walk properly
Mrs S. Elliott — face hit by flying glass, not serious
David Elliott (14) — arm injured, cried
VW Beetle passengers :-
Mr Richard Ward — leg broken, unable to move
Mrs S. Ward — broken nose, very upset
Lucy Ward (15) — hand cut open, not badly
Both vehicles badly damaged. Traffic delayed 30 minutes.
```

Use the notes to write about the accident. Use passive forms with "get" wherever possible. Begin like this:

The driver of the Mini was called Don Elliott. His left knee got hurt so that he was unable to walk properly. His wife's face ..., but ... .

Go on. Add any details you consider interesting.

4 Make up the conversations taking place in these pictures.

film/develop/Friday   clothes/wash/tomorrow   trousers/clean/weekend

shoes/repair/Saturday   engine/look at/lunch time   cassette recorder/check
                                                    and clean/next Monday

1. *Customer:* Good morning. I'd like this film developed please.
   Assistant: Certainly, sir. Will Saturday be OK for you?
   Customer: Well, I'd really like it done by Friday, if you don't mind.
   Assistant: We'll do our best, but I'm afraid I can't promise.
2. *Customer:* ... washed please.   *Go on.*

5 -ing forms (gerunds) – active and passive

Which is nicer?

1. If you give somebody a present, or if somebody gives *you* one?
   Well, I think *being given* a present is nicer than *giving* one.
2. To tell jokes yourself, or to be told them by other people?
   In my opinion *telling jokes* is nicer than ... them.
3. If you're visited by friends, or if you visit friends yourself?
   Personally/As far as I'm concerned/If you ask me, ...
4. To be taken out to a restaurant, or to cook a meal yourself?
5. To ask a girl/boy to dance, or to be asked to dance by a girl/boy?
6. If you're shown somebody else's holiday slides, or if you show your own?

6 -ing forms (gerunds) – active and passive

Complete this TV interview by putting in either an -ing form, or a preposition, or a preposition + -ing form.
Be careful: the -ing forms may be active or passive.

TV: Prime Minister, why aren't your economic politics more successful? Why aren't you getting us out of the mess we're in?
PM: Our policies *are* successful. We're making a good job *of getting* this country out of the mess left by the last government. We want to improve our economic position, and we're working hard *at improving* it all the time.
TV: But you've asked people to accept a lower standard of living. They don't like ... to do that, do they?
PM: Yes, I asked people to do that, and I apologize ... ... them to do that. Of course, I could promise better things instead. But it's no good ... to give people lots of good things and then not ... them what they were promised. I prefer to tell the truth. People aren't afraid ... ... the truth, you know.
TV: The newspapers have criticized you a lot. Do you mind ... by the press?
PM: Not at all. Politicians are used *to* people *criticizing* them. But I do like to be reported correctly. I'm fed up ... the press ... things that I've never said at all. And some papers really do mislead the public. I have strong feelings ... people ... by the press in this way.
TV: Prime Minister, do you think you'll win the next election, or are you in danger ... ... it?
PM: We shall win of course. I'm not afraid ... ... at all. I'm looking forward ... ... Prime Minister for a few more years.

2 English G 6 A

17

7 *Look at these three ways of answering a question about the future.*

Will a Channel tunnel ever be built between England and France? –
a) Yes, I think it *will* be built, as trade between Britain and Europe is growing and will make the tunnel even more necessary than it is now.
b) No, in my opinion a tunnel *will not (won't)* be built because it would be too expensive.
c) I don't know. It *may* be built since more and more people and goods have to cross the Channel, but there *may not* be enough money to build it.

Make use of these different forms in discussing the following questions. Afterwards write down your own opinion.

1. Will there be any oil left in the year 2000? – 2. Will computers soon replace teachers? – 3. Will supersonic passenger planes be common in 20 years? – 4. Will human beings ever land on another planet? – 5. Will there be a world government by the year 2500? – 6. Will we be able to control the weather in the next century? – 7. Will you live to 100?

8 be to

1. *Secretary (to Miss Bates):* Mr Williams says you're to stay longer.
2. *Applicant:* So I ... in London on May 2nd for an interview.
3. *Mrs Kelly (to husband):* Charles, you ... wear a black tie, and I ... .
4. *Mr Bean (to wife):* The notice says we ... for the theatre trip.
5. *Bank robber:* Nobody ... till I say so!
6. *Sally (to brother):* When ..., Simon? Ten or half past?
7. *Teacher (to pupil):* Will you please tell Smith that he ... .
8. *Editor (to boss):* ... this Sunday or not?

9 Reported speech – direct speech

Here is part of a story about some policemen in Chicago.

Willis asked the other two policemen to come into his office for a minute. Curtis agreed, as long as Willis did not take too long. Fasati pointed out that he would like to get his lunch soon.
Willis told them to sit down and shut the door. He offered a cigarette, which Curtis refused and Fasati accepted. Willis wanted to know what they were going to do about the bank raids. Fasati thought they ought to arrest Olson at once. Willis advised them to find some more evidence first – there was not enough to convince a court. Curtis suggested that Olson should be followed, but Fasati reckoned this was too dangerous – he might realize what was happening. Willis agreed but added that they really had to have more evidence before they could arrest Olson. He told them to go out and find some. Curtis said they would do their best. Fasati thought it would not be the easiest job they had ever had.

Imagine you have to write the dialogue for a film. There are, of course, several different ways of writing it. Here are some ways to start.

Willis: Would you two come into my office for a minute, please?   *or*
May I ask you two to come ...?   *or*
I wonder if you two would mind coming ....
Curtis: OK/All right/That's fine as long as you don't ....   *Go on.*

*10 must – have got to

Mr and Mrs O'Neill from Miami, Florida, are on their first visit to London. They're sometimes a little surprised at the things they're asked to do.

1. Mr O'Neill (at airport): We've got to wait half an hour for our luggage, I'm afraid, dear.
2. Official (at theatre): Sorry, madam. All bags must be searched.
3. Mr O'Neill (at bank): Where's my passport, dear? I ... show it.
4. Mrs O'Neill (at museum): I thought museums were free but it seems we ... pay.
5. Attendant (at museum): Umbrellas ... be left at the entrance, sir.
6. Museum keeper: I'm sorry, madam, but I ... ask you to keep quiet in the museum.
7. Ticket inspector: Excuse me, sir. If you want to smoke, you ... go in the next carriage.
8. Mrs O'Neill (at station): Tickets out, dear. We ... show them at the barrier.

1 Ex

11 Some modals

Read this conversation:

Alan: ⒶShall we go fishing this afternoon?
Derek: Well, I Ⓑshould do some wallpapering really. I'm supposed to be decorating my bedroom, you see.
Alan: But you Ⓒneedn't do it this afternoon, Ⓒneed you?
Derek: Well, I think I'd better actually.

For the expressions Ⓐ, Ⓑ and Ⓒ, you can choose alternatives from this list.

Ⓐ Shall we/Would you like to
Ⓑ should/ought to
Ⓒ needn't ... need/haven't got to ... have

Now make use of these alternatives and complete these conversations.

1. Linda: ... meet at the coffee-bar tomorrow morning?
   Norman: Well, I ... go to the Job Centre really. I'm supposed to be looking for a job, you see.
   Linda: But you ... go there tomorrow morning, ... you?
   Norman: Well, I think I ... actually.

2. Jerry: ... go to the match after school today?
   Janet: ... go down to the party office ... delivering leaflets ... .
   Jerry: But ... after school today, ...?
   Janet: ...

3. Susie: ... watch the play on TV tonight?
   Marcia: ... do some homework ... working for my A-levels ... .
   Susie: ...
   Marcia: ...

Rev.

12

Here are four road signs with their meanings:

 You must keep left.
 You mustn't stop here.
 You can park here.
 There may be rocks on the road ahead.

Use one of these modals to give the meaning of each of the following:

1
2
3
4
5
6
7
8
9
10

Rev.

20

13 Phrasal verbs in the passive

> *Don't forget that English verbs with a preposition or adverb (phrasal verbs) can also be used in the passive.*
>
> 1. They picked all the rubbish up and got rid of it in just 10 minutes.
>   All the rubbish **was picked up** and **got rid of** in just 10 minutes.
> 2. We'll have to deal with this problem first.
>   This problem will have to **be dealt with** first.

Dr Wing is a psychiatrist. He tries hard to understand his patients' problems.

1. *Patient:* My husband never talks to me.
   Dr Wing: But everyone wants to be *talked to* sometimes.
2. *Patient:* And if he does talk, he argues with me all the time. I hate it.
   Dr Wing: Of course. Anyone would hate to be … all the time.
3. *Patient:* Too true. Or he grumbles at me the whole time. I can't stand it.
   Dr Wing: Well, I couldn't stand it either if I … .
4. *Patient:* Mmmm, I see you're getting the picture. And, you know, he never listens to me when I speak – though I'd certainly prefer him to.
   Dr Wing: I can understand that you'd prefer to … .
5. *Patient:* You're really quick, I must say. – And here's another thing: he just laughs at me. Would *you* like that?
   Dr Wing: Of course I wouldn't … . No one would.
6. *Patient:* How right you are! And what's more, he looks down on me all the time. It's awful.
   Dr Wing: I can see how awful it is for you to … .
7. *Patient:* Doctor, you're so clever. You understand everything. Do you know my husband never cheers me up when I'm unhappy?
   Dr Wing: Well, I can understand that you want … .
8. *Patient:* What a wonderful psychiatrist you are! – He never even takes me out, although I'd like him to.
   Dr Wing: But of course you'd like … sometimes. That's obvious.
9. *Patient:* Yes, like everything else you say. – My husband never takes care of me when I'm ill. What do you say to that?
   Dr Wing: I can appreciate that you want … . I really can.
10. *Patient:* That's just great. I'm so glad I came to see you. – My husband ought to look after me properly. That's what I need!
    Dr Wing: Of course, of course. We all need …, don't we?
    Patient: Oh, I agree with you there – that's why I need a new psychiatrist. Good-bye, Dr Wing.

Rev.

1 Ex

14 Vocabulary

Sometimes it's better to use a different word than the same one twice. Replace the repeated word in the sentences by one of the following:

boring – candidates – completely – defeated – fortunately – frequently – injured – lately – nearly – normally – opportunity – permitted – suitable – view

1. The President expressed his opinion on the world trade situation, and then listened to the Prime Minister's opinion.
2. The economy has been improving recently. Just recently the government seems to have got prices under control.
3. Britain suggested May 20th as a convenient date but the French thought May 9th would be more convenient.
4. Seven people were hurt in the explosion and three firemen were hurt while fighting the fire.
5. Mr Milner is usually protected by two policemen who usually ride on motor-bikes behind his car.
6. Luckily there were no passengers on the train at the time of the crash, and luckily the driver was able to reduce speed.
7. School leavers must be given the chance to learn useful skills; they all ought to have the chance to train for a job.
8. Mr Benn often says silly things which often cause arguments.
9. The policy has been totally successful and the gang has been totally destroyed.
10. Visitors to the prison are allowed to bring a parcel, but they aren't allowed to bring food.
11. Leeds almost scored when Hill almost put the ball in his own goal.
12. It was a dull game, though not so dull as the one on Wednesday.
13. There are four applicants for the job of team manager. All the applicants are with other top clubs.
14. At Wimbledon yesterday the American Wagner beat Britain's Dave Lee, and Germany's Becker beat the Italian Mario De Lorenzo.

Rev.

Interpreting

1 If you don't know a word in English and you can't think of a suitable German equivalent, you must try and express yourself in another way. Suppose you don't know the word for "Wagenheber". You could paraphrase it like this: "A tool/a thing/something to lift cars with. Do you know what I mean?"

Quite often English people will tell you the word you didn't know and might say something like this:

"Oh yes, you mean 'jack', don't you?"

Interpreting   **1** [Ex]

2   In this situation at a camping site the interpreter uses this technique.

   German boy (to stranger): Entschuldigen Sie mal, könnte ich vielleicht Ihren
                       Wagenheber borgen?
   Englishman: I'm sorry, I don't understand German.
   Interpreter: The boy needs a .... I'm sorry I don't know the proper word.
                       It's a kind of tool to lift cars with. Do you know what I mean?
   Englishman: But of course, he wants a jack. Tell him to come with me.

3   The following examples show some ways of paraphrasing nouns for which
   you may not know equivalents.

   a) Wiege (cot) –   a kind of bed for a baby
      Rasenmäher (lawn-mower) –   a machine for cutting grass
      Düngemittel (fertilizer) –   something used for making land fertile
      Tauchsieder (immersion heater) – an electric thing that you can put in a
                                        cup to make water hot

   b) Schneider (tailor) –   somebody/a person who makes clothes
      Schlosser (locksmith) –   a person you need when you've lost a key
      Witwe (widow) –   a woman whose husband has died

   c) Garderobe (cloakroom) –   a place where hats, coats, etc. may be left
      Speisekammer (larder) –   a small room in which food is kept

4   Now paraphrase the following nouns by using the above patterns.

   a) Nähmaschine, Locher, Geschirrspülmaschine, Ventilator, Verstärker,
      Regenmantel, Schlafanzug, Blechschere
      Sonnenschutzcreme, Backpulver, Insektenpulver, Tränengas, Mäusegift,
      Haarwaschmittel, Schlafmittel, Beruhigungsmittel
      Lippenstift, Fön, Badetuch, Postanweisung, Ratenzahlung, Arbeitslosen-
      unterstützung, Rente, Orgel

   b) Augenarzt, Kinderärztin, Installateur, Rentner, Ladendieb, Junggeselle

   c) Scheune, Speisewagen, Gepäckaufbewahrung, Fundbüro, Treibhaus,
      Vereinslokal, Wüste

5   Now play this interpreting game: Pupil A chooses one of the nouns from the
   lists in § 4 and imagines a suitable situation where it might be used. Pupil B
   is the interpreter. Example:

   A: Kannst du mal fragen, wo es zum Fundbüro geht?
   B: Excuse me, this boy/girl would like to know the way to the – um – I don't
       know the right word for it. It's the place where things are kept that people
       have found. Do you know what I'm trying to say?

   Instead of "I don't know the right word for it" you can also say:
   "What's it called?/How can I put it?/How can I explain it?"

1 Ex

Communication practice: *Reproaching people and reacting to reproaches*

1 Jeff borrowed his sister's cassette recorder for the weekend. On Monday when he gave it back, it didn't work any more.

  Nancy: What on earth have you been doing with my recorder? It's broken.
  Jeff: Really? I'm terribly sorry, Nancy. But it was working properly on Saturday when I had it with me on the beach.
  Nancy: On the beach? Oh no! It's probably full of sand. How often must I tell you to be more careful with my things? I won't lend you anything ever again.
  Jeff: Okay, I admit it. It was a stupid thing to do and I should have known better. Give it to me. I'll try to have it repaired.

2 In the above situation Nancy reproaches Jeff for being careless. He apologizes and admits the blame. Here are some useful phrases:

a) *for reproaching people*	b) *for apologizing*
What on earth/in the world ... ?	I'm (very/terribly/awfully) sorry ...
How often must I tell you ... ?	Okay, I admit it.
I told you (not) to ...	All right, it was my mistake.
You should(n't) have ...	It's all my fault.
It's your fault that/if ...	It was a stupid thing to ...
You've really messed up ...	I'd like to apologize for ...
Don't you know better than to ... ?	I should have known better than to ...

3 But suppose Jeff thought it wasn't his fault. He could have said:

  Jeff: Look, don't blame me. It isn't my fault. I was really very careful with the thing. It's just a bit old, isn't it?

  If you don't accept the blame, you must try and justify yourself. Here are some useful phrases to use when you want *to justify yourself*:

Look, don't blame me.	Nobody told me ...
Now look here a moment, ...	How am I supposed to know ... ?
It isn't my fault, you know.	I can't/couldn't help it if ...
That's not true at all.	Look, can't you understand ... ?

4 Choose phrases from 2 and 3 and complete the following dialogues:

  a) Brian Colman (16) drove his father's car into the garage last night and forgot to turn the lights off. Now Brian's father can't start the car.

  Mr Colman (reproaches Brian for leaving the lights on): ... .
  Brian (apologizes): ... . (was tired/didn't notice)

Communication practice

b) Susan Moore gave a party for her teenage friends while her parents were away. When they returned, they found the house in a mess and a neighbour complained that it had been noisy.

Mrs Moore (blames Susan for the mess): ... .
Susan (justifies herself): ... . (tried to be careful/promises to clear up)
Mr Moore (mentions neighbour's complaint about the noise): ... .
Susan (rejects reproach): ... . (impossible to dance without music)

5   Now develop short dialogues for the following situations:

1. Harold (15) has got a Saturday job at a supermarket. One day some ice-cream was delivered which Harold forgot to put in the fridge. Now the manager has noticed it and is angry with Harold, who apologizes and promises that it won't happen again.

2. The Jacksons have arrived at their seaside resort in Spain and discovered that they've left their traveller's cheques at home. They blame each other for forgetting them.

3. Mr and Mrs Evans have gone out for the evening. Jane Evans (15) and her brother Martin (16) are at home. Martin is watching TV while Jane is preparing dinner. She leaves the kitchen to answer the phone and when she returns ten minutes later, the sausages are burned. Jane blames her brother for not looking after them. Martin justifies himself.

4. The school basketball team has lost an important game because Tommy Green, the star player, tried to make baskets on his own from impossible positions instead of passing the ball to other players in better positions. After the game the coach reproaches Tommy, who justifies himself.

5. After a school party where Tony (18) and some other older pupils got drunk, the headmaster made a rule that alcoholic drinks would no longer be allowed at school parties. Tony is blamed by some of his classmates for this decision, but he rejects their reproaches. He points out that the head has wanted such a rule for a long time anyway, and besides he wasn't the only one who got drunk.

1 S

1 The passive

a with "say", "think", "believe", etc. + infinitive with "to"

People/They say that the President drinks too much.
It's said that the President drinks too much.

As you know, the passive is often used when the subject of an active sentence is not very important or interesting. With *say, think, believe, suppose, expect, know, consider* and *report* the following passive pattern is very common:

The President	**is said**	**to** drink too much. (... soll angeblich ...)
Mr Harding	**isn't considered**	by most people **to** be suitable. (... soll nach Ansicht der meisten Leute nicht ...)
Three people	**are believed**	**to** have died in the accident.
The exhibition	**is supposed**	**to** be going on for another month.

b with "get" instead of "be"

After the accident his arm was broken.. (a state: „war gebrochen")
His arm was broken in the accident.
His arm **got broken** in the accident. } (an action: „wurde gebrochen")

In informal English, *get* is sometimes used instead of *be* in passive sentences. It <u>refers to</u> an action, not a state.

c "want/would like" + object + past participle

I want/would like **you to clean** this jacket, please.
I want/would like **this jacket to be cleaned**, please.

We already know that *want* and *would like* can be followed by an object + infinitive with *to*: either the active infinitive (*clean*, as in the first sentence) or the passive infinitive (*be cleaned*, as in the second sentence). In sentences with the passive infinitive you can leave out the words *to be* and just use the past participle:

I want/would like **this jacket** (to be) **cleaned**, please.
Do you want/Would you like **the trousers cleaned**, too?

d -ing form (gerund) in the passive

What do you prefer – driving or **being driven**?
Jones is leading, but he's in danger of **being overtaken** by Barlow.

The passive gerund (*being* + past participle) is used in the same way as the active gerund.

2 More about modals and auxiliaries

a may

I'm not sure, but it **may**/might rain. – He **may**/might be sleeping.
May in direct speech becomes *might* in reported speech:
Tom: I **may** be late. – Tom said he **might** be late.

b "be to" (for instructions)

You**'re to** listen carefully.   Nobody **is to** leave until the police say so.
Sie sollen ...   Niemand darf ...

Sally: When **are we to** be back? – *Bob:* We**'re to** be back by 10, Mother said.
Sally asked when they **were to** be back.

A form of the verb *be* + infinitive with *to* can be used to give or ask about instructions. It's often used when the instructions come from somebody else, not the speaker himself.

(c)⁺ "be to" (for arrangements)

Mrs Smith (to husband): Oh, the Queen is visiting the U.S.A. next month.
Radio news: The Queen **is to** visit the U.S.A. next month.
　　　　　　　　... wird ...

A form of *be* + infinitive with *to* can also be used to show that something has been arranged. It's especially common in formal contexts.
Note: in newspaper headlines the verb *be* is often left out to save space:
　　QUEEN TO VISIT U.S.A. NEXT MONTH

(d) "shall" and "should" for "will" and "would" in the 1st person

I **shall** read the book first. – We **should** appreciate an early reply.
Shall and *should* are often used in more formal English (written or spoken).
Note: the negative short form of *shall* is *shan't* [ʃɑːnt].

(e) "will" and "would" for habits and typical behaviour

Jane | sits and reads | magazines for hours.
　　　| **will** sit and read |
When I was little, I | often played | happily on my own.
　　　　　　　　　　| **would** often play |

Will + infinitive is sometimes used instead of the simple present when talking about somebody's habits or typical behaviour.
Similarly, *would* + infinitive can be used instead of the simple past.

⁺Die grammatikalischen Erscheinungen der eingeklammerten Abschnitte brauchen nicht aktiv verwendet zu werden.

Revision

3 Modals: some ways of expressing obligation

a have (got) to

I'm sorry, I've really got to go now./I really have to go now.
Where do I have to put my signature/have I got to put my signature?
Bob has (got) to start work at 7.30.

Have to is the usual form in American English (AE); in British English (BE) both forms are common.

b must

I'm sorry, I really must go now.
Don't forget, you must be back by 2 o'clock.
Umbrellas must be left at the entrance.
You needn't buy more toothpaste – I bought some yesterday.
Players must not touch the ball with their hands.

Must has two different negative forms: *needn't* and *mustn't*.
Remember: *needn't* = it's not necessary,
            mustn't = it's not allowed.
Must has no regular past/future forms; *had to/will have to* are used instead.

Yesterday I had to get up at 6 to catch the early train.
Tomorrow my sister will have to do the shopping for the weekend.

(c) "have (got) to" – "must" in contrast

We really have to go now. (Our train leaves in 20 minutes.)
I really must go now. (I feel it's my duty.)

With *I* and *we* (the first person), *have (got) to* emphasizes that the speaker feels obliged by circumstances outside his control; *must* emphasizes that the speaker feels a sense of duty.

You've got to be back by 2. (That's what the boss said.)
You must be back by 2. (That's an order from me.)
Have you heard about Susan's party? Everybody has to bring a record.
Susan: I've had a good idea for my party – everybody must bring a record.

With the second and third person, *have (got) to* is preferred if the speaker is talking about an order given by somebody else; *must* is preferred if the speaker himself is giving an order.

d be to

Mr P. Smith is the man I'm to see for my interview.
Don't forget what Mother said: you're to be back by 10.
The lady asked where she was to put her signature on the paper.

Be to is used to give orders or instructions (usually not the speaker's own). It's less strong than *have (got) to* or *must*.

e ought to / should

I really **ought to**/**should** go now, but I think I'll stay a little longer.
I think she **ought to**/**should** sell her car and buy a smaller one.
You **ought to**/**should** have spoken to me about the problem earlier.

Ought to/should are weaker than *have (got) to, must* or *be to*.

f be supposed to

Prime Ministers **are supposed to** behave in a responsible way.
Oh dear, it's already 7.55 and we're supposed to be there at 8.
Tom was supposed to meet me at the cinema, but he completely forgot.

Be supposed to expresses a rather weak obligation — either a duty or an arrangement.

Unit 2 A

1 Mandarin – a form of Chinese – is spoken as a first (or native) language by more people than any other in the world. However, few people outside China have any knowledge of it, and not everybody inside China uses it either. With English it's different. The population of England is about 46 million, yet there are an estimated 369 million people throughout the world who speak English as their native language.

The top ten native languages of the world

Language	Country	Millions
1. Mandarin	China	670
2. English	U.K., U.S.A., etc.	369
3. Hindi-Urdu	India, Pakistan	278
4. Russian	U.S.S.R.	246
5. Spanish	Spain, Mexico, etc.	225
6. Arabic	Egypt, Saudi Arabia, etc.	134
7. Portuguese	Portugal, Brazil, etc.	133
8. Bengali	Bangladesh, India	131
9. German	Germany (West + East), Austria, Switzerland, etc.	120
10. Japanese	Japan	113

● What other countries can you think of where English is spoken as a native language? Find out as many as you can.

2 In addition to the 369 million people who speak English as their native language, it's estimated that a similar number of people – probably at least 400 million – speak it as a second or foreign language. English is a second language for those who live in countries where it's used for some official purposes, e.g. in schools, universities or courts (India, Pakistan, Hong Kong, Singapore and a number of African states); otherwise, in countries where it has no such official status, it's a foreign language (Germany, France, Japan, etc.).

It's impossible to say exactly how many people throughout the world are, at this moment, learning English as a foreign language, but in West Germany alone there are roughly 5 million pupils aged 11-18 and most of them are learning English – including you!

● English is the international language of the air – that's one reason people learn English. What other reasons can you think of? Ex 12

3   400 years ago, all English-speaking people lived in the British Isles. Only about 1 in 100 of the world's population used English; today it's used by about 1 in 7 people throughout the world. Two of the main reasons for this remarkable development are the following:

– The British Empire was built up **providing** Britain with colonies all over the world. (Remember that the U.S.A. started as a British colony!)

– Especially since the end of the Second World War the U.S.A. has grown enormously in world-wide influence, **playing** a leading role in such fields as science, technology and, last but not least, pop culture[1].   S 2 · Ex 5, 6

4   English has had an influence on other languages too. Think of all the English words that have gradually become acceptable in German, such as:

boss, manager, teenager, party, bestseller, hit, popsong, filmstar, NATO (North Atlantic Treaty Organization).

• Go on and make your own list of English words or expressions that have been taken over by German. What areas of life do most of them come from? Arrange them in groups, e.g. food, pop, business, organizations, etc.

5   When German **takes over** English words, it sometimes changes their meaning or **puts** two words **together** to make a new one that doesn't exist in English. Here are some examples:

'German' English	British English equivalent
clever	smart, sharp (clever = begabt, klug, geschickt)
City	city centre (city = Großstadt)
Slip	pants/panties (slip = Unterrock)
Smoking	dinner-jacket (the word "smoking-jacket" is no longer used)
Dressman	male model (the word "dressman" doesn't exist)
Evergreen	popular old song, "oldie" (evergreen = a kind of tree)
Musikbox	juke-box (music/musical box = Spieldose)
Oldtimer	veteran car (oldtimer = old person with long experience)
Gag	gimmick (gag = a kind of joke)
Showmaster	host, compère (the word "showmaster" doesn't exist)

S 1a, b · Ex 1–4

6   So far English has been spoken of as if it was one and the same language throughout the world. But that's not true of course. American English is, as you know, different from British English in a number of ways. In pronunciation, for example. That's what makes this joke possible:

American: What kind of work do you do?
Englishman: I'm a clerk.
American: A clock?
Englishman: Yes, a clerk. What's so funny about that?
American: You mean you just go tick-tock, tick-tock?

[1] In ENGLISH Project Book 3: A COMMON LANGUAGE you can read poems, short stories and newspaper articles from many different countries in which English is spoken, e.g. Canada, India, South Africa, Tanzania, Trinidad.

7 But American English is not the only kind of English that is different from British English; so is the English spoken in South Africa, Australia, India, the West Indies and every other English-speaking country. Even where spelling, vocabulary and grammar are not very different, pronunciation and intonation are usually enough for most people to recognize where the speaker comes from[1].

Ever heard of "pidgin" English?

One kind of English that's thoroughly different from the language spoken in Britain and the U.S.A. is pidgin, or pidgin English. Pidgin is spoken in different parts of the world (e.g. West Africa, Hawaii and New Guinea). It's a mixture between English and the particular native languages of the area. The vocabulary is mostly English, the spelling and grammar are usually rather different. Here are some examples, just for fun:

Klokbelo
Loliwara
Mama bilong skru

8 Not only **do different countries have** their own varieties of English, there are also different varieties of the language within each country. Let's take the U.K. Apart from Welsh (spoken by 542,400 people in 1971) and the Gaelic languages of the Scots and Irish (spoken by some 100,000 people), many different accents and dialects of English can be heard.

S 3a, (b) · Ex 8, 9

9 As far as accent is concerned, it's the vowel sounds that vary most in the different parts of the country. One of the biggest differences is between the south and the north of England, where the southern sounds [æ], [ɑː] and [ʌ] are pronounced [a], [æ] and [u]. Here is an example of a sentence with these vowel sounds:

Catch the fast bus.
[kætʃ ðə ˈfɑːst bʌs]   (pronunciation in the south)
[katʃ ðə ˈfæst bus]   (pronunciation in the north)

10 A dialect is different from the standard language in pronunciation but also in grammar and vocabulary. Most speakers of really broad dialects live in rural areas and so it's not surprising that farm vocabulary, especially, can vary a lot from one dialect region to another. For example, the standard word for the building where cows are kept is *cow-house* or *cow-shed,* but in the south-west it's known as a *shippon,* in the north-east as a *byre,* and in various other parts as a *beast-house, neat-house, cow-stable* and *mistall.*

[1]Examples of several different varieties of English are included on the Text-Cassette (Bestell-Nr. 8428) and Text-Tonband (Bestell-Nr. 8916).

11 As far as grammar is concerned, one of the most common differences between the standard language and dialects is in the use of pronouns, particularly in some of the western counties of England. Can you understand these words from a gravestone in Herefordshire?

12 Foreign visitors to Britain are often surprised to discover that London taxi-drivers don't all speak standard English, let alone like BBC newsreaders. London is, in fact, the home of Britain's most famous dialect – Cockney. Although not all working-class Londoners speak broad Cockney, many do speak in a way that makes it quite difficult for foreigners to understand. Cockney has a rich vocabulary of slang – rhyming slang, for example – as well as changes in vowel sounds, use of pronouns and certain verb forms.

> 1. *Standard English:* He hasn't ever got any time.
>   *Cockney:* 'E ain't never got no toim. [ˈiː ein ˈnevə gɔ nəau ˈtɔim]
> 2. *Standard English:* I fell down those stairs.
>   *Cockney:* Oi fell dahn them apples 'n' pears. [ɔi fel ˈdɑːn ðem ˈæplzn ˈpəːz]

13 It isn't always socially acceptable to speak with a regional accent in Britain. Many British people are still very conscious of whether somebody is working-class or middle-class, and speaking with a regional accent is often considered not proper for educated middle-class people. If you **should** happen to come from a part of Britain with a distinct local accent, you might have to give it up. This would be necessary in order to be accepted as, say, a doctor or a lawyer, or to be promoted to the top jobs in the civil service or the army. For people with such career plans it is advisable to acquire the regionally neutral accent of newsreaders on radio or television: BBC English. A slight accent may be accepted as tolerable, but a broad one would make a bad impression and would almost certainly be an obstacle in such careers. In this respect Britain is different from Germany.

There is perhaps another interesting difference between Britain and Germany too. Although the majority of West Germans (57%) are said to speak a dialect fluently, most of them can also speak a kind of Hochdeutsch. Being "bilingual" in this way is not at all unusual for Germans; for the British, however, it's very unusual.

S 4a, b, (c) · Ex 13a, b, c

> "If you try hard, you can speak as good as any Englishman, though you're a Cockney. If you speak posh you have more chance of a job; if you speak Cockney you get a dirty job, a barrow-boy and that sort of thing."
>
> (18-year-old London shop assistant)
>
> **posh** (slang) *wie die feinen Leute*   **barrow-boy** *Straßenhändler*

2

*Where does English come from?

A lot of English words are easy for Germans to learn as they are so similar in both languages. But this is true for other groups of foreign learners too, because there are words in their languages that are equally similar. Here are some examples from French, Swedish, Danish and Spanish:

gouvernement, skinn, educación, rivière, liv, kniv, arriver, persuadir, défendre, ambicioso, træ, lengua.

What are the reasons for this? To find out, it is necessary to go back a long way in British history. –

2000 years ago the people who lived on the island now called Britain were Celts, and they spoke a variety of Celtic dialects. In 55 BC the first Romans arrived from across the Channel, bringing with them their own language: Latin. The Romans stayed in Britain for over 400 years but only a very few Latin words were taken over by the Celts and still survive today – place names mostly.

Not many years after the last Romans had left, Britain was invaded by the Angles, Saxons and Jutes – three Germanic tribes speaking similar dialects. Unlike the Romans, these people forced the Celts to quit their homes and settle in the extreme west and north of Britain. Anglo-Saxon replaced Celtic as the native language, the name "English" coming from the Angles. During the 9th century, Vikings – Norwegians and Danes – began to settle in Britain, which led of course to new influences on the native language, but basically it was still Anglo-Saxon. At the same time, many Latin words were entering the language as a result of the Christianization of the country.

It was the Norman Conquest of 1066 that had the greatest influence on English. For nearly 300 years French was the official language in England, but the native population continued to speak Anglo-Saxon. French was finally given up as an official language in the 14th century, but many French words had been taken over by that time.

At the end of the 15th century there were still several different dialects spoken in England, but it was the use of London English in parliament, law, documents, schools and poetry that led to the formation of a standard language. This development was reinforced when the first printing press was opened in London by William Caxton in 1476. 100 years later the dialect of London and the East Midlands had become accepted as the standard form of English. And although pronunciation, vocabulary and grammar have changed quite a lot over the past 500 years, spelling has changed very little. That is why, today, the written form of a word is often no help to a foreign learner in knowing how to pronounce it. Compare the pronunciation of the letter "o" in these words:

over, lost, lose, London, more, woman, women.

2 T2

It's nice, isn't it?

When I arrived in England I thought I knew English. After I'd been here an hour I realized that I did not understand one word. In the first week I picked up a tolerable working knowledge of the language and the next seven years convinced me gradually but thoroughly that I would never know it really well, let alone perfectly. This is sad. My only consolation being that nobody speaks English perfectly.

Remember that those five hundred words an average Englishman uses are far from being the whole vocabulary of the language. You may learn another five hundred and another five thousand and yet another five thousand and still you may come across a further fifty thousand you have never heard of before, and nobody else either.

If you live here long enough you will find out to your greatest amazement that the adjective *nice* is not the only adjective the language possesses, in spite of the fact that in the first three years you do not need to learn or use any other adjectives. You can say that the weather is nice, a restaurant is nice, Mr So-and-so is nice, Mrs So-and-so's clothes are nice, you had a nice time, and all this will be very nice.

... The easiest way to give the impression of having a good accent or no foreign accent at all is to hold an unlit pipe in your mouth, to mutter between your teeth and finish all your sentences with the question: "isn't it?" People will not understand much, but they are accustomed to that and they will get a most excellent impression.

... Finally, there are two important points to remember:
1. Do not forget that it is much easier to write in English than to speak English, because you can write without a foreign accent.
2. In a bus and in other public places it is more advisable to speak softly in good German than to shout in abominable English.

Anyway, this whole language business is not at all easy. After spending eight years in this country, the other day I was told by a very kind lady: "But why do you complain? You really speak a most excellent accent without the slightest English."

(From *How to be an Alien* by George Mikes)

- 1. Does the writer think English is easy or difficult to learn? Find sentences which support your arguments.
  2. What does the text say about accents?
  3. What advice does Mikes give those who want to speak good English? What do you think of his suggestions?
  4. Which German equivalent would you suggest for the adjective "nice"?
  5. Mikes says a number of things which are not, strictly speaking, true. Find examples. What does he hope to achieve by doing this?

There was a young ...

Both in Britain and America the limerick has a long tradition as a popular form of funny verse. It generally follows strict rules: its five lines have the rhyme pattern a-a-b-b-a, the 'a' lines each with three stressed syllables, the 'b' lines each with two. Within these five lines a story is told about a character introduced in the first line. The best limericks make us laugh by providing a clever or surprise ending in the last line, like this one:

There was a young lady named Bright,
Whose speed was much faster than light;
    She set off one day
    In a relative way,
And returned the previous night.

A number of tricks may be used to give a limerick extra 'spice'. For example, the rules of rhyme or stress may be broken, or spelling tricks used:

There was a young man of Japan,
Who wrote verses that never would scan;
    When asked why this was,
    He said: "It's because
I always try to get as many syllables
into the last line as I possibly can."

scan *Rhythmus haben*

She got mad and called him "Mr",
Not because he came and kr,
    But because, just before,
    As he stood at the door,
This Mr kr sr.

A remarkable bird is the pelican,
His beak holds more than his belican;
    He can take in his beak
    Enough food for a week —
But I'm damned if I know how the helican.

beak *Schnabel*   belly *Bauch*

Another favourite trick is to play with the different meanings of words:

There was a young girl of West Ham,
Who smiled as she jumped on a tram;
    As she quickly embarked
    The conductor remarked,
"Your fare, Miss." She said, "Yes, I am."

tram *Straßenbahn*   embark *einsteigen*
You're fair = You're beautiful

There was a young fellow named Hall,
Who fell in the spring in the fall;
    It would have been a sad thing
    Had he died in the spring,
But he didn't — he died in the fall.

spring *Frühling / Sprung / Quelle*
fall   *Herbst / Sturz / Wasserfall*

Finally, here's an unfinished limerick. Can you make up a good last line?

Lots of students in West Germany
Use a textbook called ENGLISH G;
    We editors hope
    You were able to cope
....

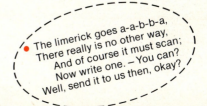

The limerick goes a-a-b-b-a,
There really is no other way,
And of course it must scan;
Now write one. — You can?
Well, send it to us then, okay?

2 Ex

1 Phrasal verbs

Put in the correct adverbs that go with the verbs in these sentences:

1. Try to calm *down*, Jenny. It's not the end of the world.
2. If the weather doesn't clear ... soon, we'll have to give ... our plan to walk to Robert's.
3. For flights to Paris, check ... at counter B 14, please.
4. Where's the notice that was on the board? Who's taken it ...?
5. Excuse me, it's so warm, do you mind if I take ... my jacket?
6. Do you know how long David has been going ... with Pamela?
7. Well done, Lucy. Keep ... the good work.
8. Hallo, Webb Motors? Can you put me ... to Mr Cook, please?
9. Have you managed to settle ... in the new neighbourhood?
10. I've already heard that side of the record. Turn it ... now, please.
11. I heard a loud noise behind me, but when I turned ..., there was nothing there.
12. If you don't like the programme, turn it ... .

2 *Put the correct form of these verbs into the following conversation:*

cheer up, find out, go on, go out, go up, make up, point out, put up with, queue up, shut up, switch on, take out, turn off, turn round, wake up, walk out, wash up

Clare: Hallo, Liz. You look a bit miserable. *Cheer up*.
Liz: It's that Nick Ogilvie. He really *turns* me *off*.
Clare: You ... somewhere with him last night, didn't you?
Liz: Unfortunately, yes. We went to see "Star Wars". First we had to ... for half an hour in the rain, and then I had to pay for myself. Nick complained that the prices had ... . He said he couldn't afford to pay for us both.
Clare: Did you enjoy the film?
Liz: No, I didn't. There were two people talking behind us, and I kept ... and telling them to ..., but they wouldn't. Nick seemed to be asleep and didn't ... until the film finished.
Clare: I'd have ... and gone home.
Liz: I don't know why I didn't. Well, then we went to Nick's place for a coffee and he immediately ... the TV to watch tennis. I ... that I wasn't interested in tennis, but it was no good. The programme ... for ages, while I got madder and madder.
Clare: Then what?
Liz: Oh, we just ... the coffee cups together. Then I went home.
Clare: Is this true – or are you ... it ...?
Liz: It's true. But I've ... what he's like now, and I certainly won't let him ... me ... again. I won't ... that sort of behaviour.

3 *Replace the underlined verbs with phrasal verbs of similar meaning. Be careful with the word order. There may be more than one correct possibility.*

1. After two weeks in London, the German group <u>left</u> for Bristol last night.
2. How long will the Liberals <u>continue</u> supporting the government?
3. The answer wasn't easy. It took them 10 minutes to <u>calculate</u> it.
4. I wonder how many more historic buildings will have to be <u>destroyed</u>?
5. "I know where Tina Spooner lives." – "How did you <u>discover</u> that?"
6. While fishing yesterday, I caught 6 fish – but two managed to <u>escape</u>.
7. Sorry, I can't <u>phone</u> Chris – I haven't got her number.
8. The speaker <u>began</u> by telling the audience a few jokes.
9. For heaven's sake, let's <u>tidy</u> this mess before the guests arrive.
10. The management <u>rejected</u> the plan twice before it was finally accepted.

4 *Use phrasal verbs to complete the following sentences:*

1. If you come across a word you don't know, you must *look it up* .
2. Your record player is far too loud, Jane. Will you please …?
3. Here's the questionnaire, Susan. After you've …, please give it to Bob.
4. Susanne was very upset when her friend Petra got such a bad report. As a result, Petra must repeat a school year. She must … .
5. Small children usually have to go to bed early. So they get excited when, for a change, they're allowed to … .
6. We'd love you to come and see us at the weekend. … at any time.
7. I'm sorry, I can't hear you. Can you please …?
8. The German visitor got injured in a fight. On his way home he was attacked by a gang and … .

5 *These pictures are part of a story in a comic. Write a sentence about each picture. Use a present participle in each sentence.*

1. Adams, a big crook in the drugs trade, sat in his car, looking at his watch.
2. Jim Boyd stood …, watching … .   3. He … .   *Go on.*

2 Ex

6 *The political party in power in Britain wants to tell people about their recent achievements. But this worker – who possibly supports a different party – has stuck the posters together wrongly.*

1. Two new motorways have been built, providing homes for over 2 million people.

2. A record 700,000 new houses have been built, earning the money we need to buy goods from other countries.

3. Britain has sold more goods abroad than ever before, improving our national road network.

4. Large amounts of money have been invested in Scottish industry, protecting Britain's interests throughout the world.

5. Welfare payments have been increased, bringing thousands of new jobs to Scotland.

6. The government has played a leading role in international affairs, making it possible for poorer families to improve their living conditions.

a *Put the six sentences together correctly.*

b *Rewrite the sentences using "which" to refer to the whole preceding clause.*

1. Two new motorways have been built, which has improved .... *Go on.*

7 a *Which English proverb goes with which German proverb?*

1. Like father, like son.	a) Was man verspricht, muß man halten.
2. Promises are made to be kept.	b) Ein gebranntes Kind scheut das Feuer.
3. You can't teach an old dog new tricks.	c) Wo gehobelt wird, da fallen Späne.
4. As you make your bed, so you must lie.	d) Vorsicht ist besser als Nachsicht.
5. Better safe than sorry.	e) Wie man sich bettet, so liegt man.
6. Out of sight, out of mind.	f) Der Apfel fällt nicht weit vom Stamm.
7. You can't make an omelette without breaking eggs.	g) Der Lauscher an der Wand hört seine eigene Schand'.
8. One swallow[1] doesn't make a summer.	h) Aus den Augen, aus dem Sinn.
9. Once bitten[2], twice shy.	i) Eine Schwalbe macht noch keinen Sommer.
10. Listeners hear no good of themselves.	j) Was Hänschen nicht lernt, lernt Hans nimmermehr.

b *Now use your own words to explain the meaning of the proverbs. Use an if-sentence each time. (Don't try to translate the German sentences!)*

1./f) If you have children, they'll probably grow up to be like you.
2./a) If someone has promised to do a thing, he should do it. *Go on.* Rev.

[1] swallow *Schwalbe*   [2] bite, I bit, I've bitten *beißen*

8 Word order: Inversion

Mr Bird has been accused of stealing £50,000 from the finance company he works for. He is being questioned in court.

1. *Lawyer:* How worried are you about your financial affairs, Mr Bird?
   Mr Bird: In no way am I. worried about my financial affairs.
2. *Lawyer:* Have you ever had serious money problems?
   Mr Bird: Hardly at all, I'd say. No, hardly ever ... .
3. *Lawyer:* How many times have you borrowed money from your company?
   Mr Bird: Not very often, I don't think. No, very few times ... .
4. *Lawyer:* You repaid the money late once, didn't you, or was it twice?
   Mr Bird: No, only ... .
5. *Lawyer:* When did you borrow as much as £10,000?
   Mr Bird: £10,000? Never. At no time ... .
6. *Lawyer:* Under what circumstances would you take money without telling the company?
   Mr Bird: Under ... .
7. *Lawyer:* In which foreign country have you got a bank account, Mr Bird?
   Mr Bird: A foreign bank account? In ... .
8. *Lawyer:* You're accused of stealing £50,000, Mr Bird. What do you say?
   Mr Bird: Complete nonsense! Never ... anything so ridiculous in my life!

9 *The Woodhouse family – Mr and Mrs Woodhouse, Barbara, Joan and Ian – have been really unlucky lately. Look at what's happened to them already this year.*

1. Mr Woodhouse found a job, but a month later the factory closed and he was unemployed again.
2. Mrs Woodhouse's wages were put up, but a fortnight later the rent went up even more.
3. Barbara started going steady with a young man at work, but then he went off to Canada.
4. Joan learned to ski, but the second time she went skiing she fell down and broke her leg.
5. Ian bought a puppy from a friend, but the next day it ran out into the road and was killed by a car.
6. They began their holiday in Scotland, but on the first day the rain came down and never stopped.

Now rewrite the sentences using "Hardly ... when" or "No sooner ... than".

1. Hardly had Mr Woodhouse found a job when the factory closed and he was unemployed again.
2. No sooner had ... than ... .   *Go on.*

2 Ex

10 If-clauses

Valerie and her friends are discussing what to do in their summer holidays. Complete their conversation, making sure you use the right tenses.

Valerie: What about camping again? That camping holiday last year was great, wasn't it? Though we should have hired a bigger tent.
Neil: Yes, if we'd hired a bigger one, we ... had more room.
Angela: And we should have practised putting it up before we set off.
Don: True. If ... putting it up at home, it ... taken us so long that first night.
Neil: What about youth hostels this year instead? We can hitch-hike if we ... want to ride our bikes again.
Angela: Oh, no. I don't like that idea. If we ..., we ... never know where we were going to spend the night.
Valerie: What about going walking in the hills?
Angela: But I want to relax and be lazy. I ... relax if we went walking. Riding that bike last year was bad enough.
Don: You ought to have had a better bike, Angela. If you ... a better one, you ... had an easier time and ... the holiday more.
Angela: Let's go abroad this year.
Neil: But if we ..., it ... very expensive, wouldn't it?
Valerie: Let's go to Scotland or Wales then.
Neil: That suits me better. If we ... there, ... a lot cheaper, won't it?
Angela: I've been to Scotland lots of times already.
Valerie: I've never been to Wales, though.
Don: Well, if Angela ... already ... to Scotland, and Valerie ... to Wales, why ... we ... to Wales then?
Neil: I can't afford to go for a fortnight this year, I'm afraid.
Don: So what? If you ... a fortnight, we ... for a week.
Angela: I'm going away with my parents the first week in August.
Valerie: And I'm staying with my aunt in the second week.
Don: OK. If Angela ... and Valerie ..., then ... third week. Does that suit everybody?
Valerie: Perfectly. I'll send away for some brochures.
Neil: Fine. If ..., we ... all ... them together at my house next week.
Angela: I'm working every evening except Thursday.
Don: OK, Angela. If ..., ... on Thursday.

Rev.

11 *Complete the following paragraph by using each of these prepositional phrases once: according to, apart from, because of, due to, except for, in addition to, in spite of, instead of*

The English language has more native speakers than any other language *apart from* Mandarin Chinese. ... recent calculations, there are 369 million people who speak English as their native language. ... these native speakers, there are hundreds of millions more using English as their second language. ... just one or two countries, English is in fact an official language throughout the Commonwealth. And why do these independent countries use English? Well, take an African country with, say, five main local languages. ... everyone learning four extra languages, it's much easier for them to learn one language – English. The world-wide use of English is partly ... the size and power of the British Empire in the 19th century. But ... the fact that the U.K. is no longer a world power, English is more than ever the world language of today. This is of course mainly ... the influence of the U.S.A.

Rev.

12 *Make a sentence about each of the pictures below, explaining why German people learn English.*
What other reasons can you think of for Germans to learn English?

1. *Pilots* and ... have to/are obliged to/need to/are required to use English, because it's the accepted international language of the air.
2. It's useful/necessary for ... to sing in English, because ... .   *Go on.*

2 Ex

13 Shirley Shaw is going out and leaving her au pair girl, Eva, and her young daughter Jill at home. These are her instructions to Eva:

1. It's just possible Mrs Dawson might ring up. If she does, tell her I'll ring back.
2. I don't think the milkman will come, but give him his money if he does.
3. Jill probably won't get hungry, but if she does, could you make her a snack, please?
4. She won't want to play outside I don't think, but take her to the park if she does.
5. I think it's warm enough, but if you're cold, switch the radiator on.
6. It's just possible Mr Black might come. Will you give him this note if he does?
7. It probably won't rain, but if it does, could you fetch the clothes in?
8. I'll try not to be late, but could you start to get the tea ready if I am?

a *Eva might have replied like this:*

1. OK. If Mrs Dawson should ring up, I'll tell her you'll ring back.
2. OK. I'll ... if he should .... *Go on.*

b *Or she might have replied like this:*

1. OK. Should Mrs Dawson ring up, I'll tell her you'll ring back.
2. OK. Should the milkman come, I'll .... *Go on.*

c *If everything had in fact happened, what would Eva have done?*

1. Had Mrs Dawson rung up, Eva would have asked her to ring back.
2. Had the milkman come, she'd have given .... *Go on.*

14 a Join each pair of sentences with a conjunction of time. Use each of the following conjunctions once only: *after, as, as soon as, before, since, until, when, while*. (Sometimes the conjunction has to go in front of the first clause, sometimes in front of the second.)

1. Young Bruce Stone was boxing in a New York club in 1944. He was spotted by boxing manager Carl Evans.
   As young Bruce Stone was boxing in ..., he was spotted by ... .
2. Evans at once decided to help Stone. He recognized his talent.
3. Stone won ten fights. Then he had to spend two years in the army.
4. He was in the army. At the same time he kept up his boxing.
5. Stone came out of the army. At once he got a chance to fight for the World Championship.
6. He was almost unknown. But not when he became Champion in 1949.
7. He defended his title eight times. He retired undefeated in 1955.
8. Stone quit boxing. He has been living quietly at his Wyoming home.

b *Rewrite the sentences as one paragraph using the following + an -ing form: after, before, on (2×), until, since, while (2×).*

Begin like this: While boxing in a New York club in 1944, Bruce .... Rev.

2 [Ex]

Interpreting

In the previous interpreting exercise you practised paraphrasing German nouns. Now here are some techniques for paraphrasing unknown adjectives.

1   Sometimes you can get close to the exact meaning of an adjective you need by taking an adjective that means roughly the same and adding an adverb like *very, quite, slightly, extremely*. Or it may be helpful to take an adjective with the opposite meaning and add *not, not quite* or *not very*:

überglücklich	*very* happy	mager	*not* fat
lauwarm	*slightly* warm	angelehnt	*not quite* closed
winzig	*extremely* small	trübe	*not very* clear

Paraphrase the following adjectives using this technique:
steinreich, ledig, abgestanden, mittelmäßig, übergroß, feucht, leichtbeschädigt, verzerrt, verarmt, angesengt, uralt, patschnaß, knochentrocken, vollschlank, bildhübsch, angeheitert

2   Many adjectives describing human beings can be paraphrased by using a verb or *have* + noun:

geschwätzig	what you say of somebody who *talks* too much
streitsüchtig	*likes* disagree*ing*/argu*ing*
obdachlos	*has* no home
barfüßig	*has* no shoes or socks on
stumm	*can*not speak

Practise this technique by using more adjectives of this kind:
kahl, gefühllos, habgierig, unersättlich, hartherzig, ungeduldig, eingebildet, gesellig, anpassungsfähig, nackt, taubstumm, trinkfest, drogenabhängig, tierlieb, kinderlos, sprachbegabt

3   The many adjectives ending in *-bar* or *-lich* may be paraphrased like this:

eßbar	something that *can be* eaten
trinkbar	*is suitable for* drinking
unvermeidlich	*cannot be* avoided
vergleichbar	*is able to be* compared
unbeschreiblich	*is unable to be* described

Use this technique to paraphrase the following adjectives:
tragbar, zerbrechlich, unausweichlich, fühlbar, unleserlich, wählbar, machbar, unmißverständlich, brauchbar, unverletzbar, unvergleichlich, wiederholbar, unwiederbringlich, unzählbar

4   Now, using these adjectives, play the interpreting game on p. 23 (§ 5).

2

Communication practice: *Hesitating*

1. Not many people can talk fluently throughout a conversation. Sometimes you can't avoid hesitating, for example when you're not sure how to express yourself. In such cases there are several ways to bridge the gap. You can use those well-known sounds "um" [əm] and "er" [əː, ʌː]. Or you can lengthen the vowel sounds of such words as "a" [eiː], "the" [ðiː] and "to" [tuː] before going on to the next word. There are, in addition, a number of helpful words and phrases that are widely used:

... well ...	... what I mean is ...
... actually ...	... what I'm trying to say is ...
... as a matter of fact ...	... the thing is ...
... you know/you see ...	... it's sort of/kind of ...
... it's like this ...	... how shall I put it? ...
... if you ask me ...	... as I say ...

2. Of course, it's best to speak as fluently as you can. But if you must hesitate, it's better to use one of these expressions than to say nothing. Here's an example:

    TV reporter: May I ask your opinion about vandalism by football fans?
    Man: Well, um, actually I was discussing this problem with, er, some of my friends, um, the other day as a matter of fact. The thing is, this is something which, er, something which has been getting worse, hasn't it? And, er, what I'm trying to say is that it's got to be, well, stopped. I reckon we've got to, as I say, be much stricter about this kind of thing, if you ask me.

3. Choose suitable expressions from 1 to fill the gaps in this conversation.

    Paul: Women drivers? ..., ... all this talk about women being rotten drivers is ... a lot of ... rubbish. It's just not true. ... I know several girls who are excellent drivers. Really. ... it's all due to ... due to ... prejudice ... .
    Gary: ... I don't think so. No, there's definitely something in it. ... women are ... different from men. – No, don't laugh. They *are*. Take Sue Harding. She looks right and left, in all the ... shop windows, everywhere except at the road ahead. ... she's ... typical ... .

4. Here are some topics for discussion. Use the techniques described in 1 whenever you feel like hesitating.

    1. Teenagers and alcoholic drinks. – 2. Violence on TV. – 3. No smoking in public places. – 4. Shorter holidays for all. – 5. Old age. – 6. My future career. – 7. Christmas. – 8. Space travel. – 9. City life.

1 Phrasal verbs (see list on p. 122)

a A phrasal verb consists of | a simple verb | + | an adverb.
e.g. *turn* | | e.g. *down*

One simple verb can go together with a number of different adverbs, e.g.:

put { **away** (wegräumen)
on (anziehen)
up (aufstellen, anschlagen)
through (durchstellen, verbinden) }

turn { **down** (leiser stellen; ablehnen)
off/on (ab-, einschalten)
over (umblättern)
round (sich umdrehen) }

Sometimes the meaning of a phrasal verb is just what you'd expect from the combination of the two parts, e.g. *write down* (niederschreiben), *turn round* (sich umdrehen), *call out* (ausrufen). But very often the phrasal verb has a new meaning, e.g. *look up* (nachschlagen), *turn down* (ablehnen), *make up* (erfinden).

b When I left, I **turned** the light **out**.
Or: When I left, I **turned out** the light.

Have you **rung** Jean **up** yet?
Or: Have you **rung up** Jean yet?

Write all the words **down** in your notebook.
Or: **Write down** all the words in your notebook.

Many phrasal verbs are transitive, i.e. they can be followed by a direct object. When the object is a noun or a short noun phrase, it can go *either* between the verb and the adverb *or* after the adverb. But:

1. when the object is a pronoun, it must go between the verb and the adverb, e.g.:

   I **turned** it **out**. – Have you **rung** her **up**? – **Write** them **down** in your book.

2. when the object is a long noun phrase or a clause, it must go after the adverb, e.g.:

   I **turned out** all the lights, the TV, the radio and the record player.
   Please **write down** what we learned yesterday.

2 More about present participles

He introduced himself, shak**ing** hands with everyone. (... indem er ...)
They left the room talk**ing** excitedly. (... wobei sie ...)
Jane sat in the living-room watch**ing** TV. (... saß ... und ...)

The -ing form (present participle) is often used in English where the German equivalent is either an adverbial clause (introduced by *indem* or *wobei*) or a second main clause (introduced by *und*).
Note the German equivalent when the -ing form is used after *come*:

He came runn**ing** into the room. (Er kam ins Zimmer gelaufen.)

3 Word order: inversion

a **He visited** the exhibition only once. (word order in statements)
Did he visit the exhibition only once? (word order in yes/no questions)
Only once **did he visit** the exhibition. (emphasis on *only once*)
Never **have I seen** such a good-looking girl.
Hardly **had we arrived** when it started raining.
No sooner **does he get up** than he makes himself a cup of tea.

A number of adverbs and adverbial phrases with a negative sense can be put at the beginning of a sentence for emphasis. They're then followed by the word order in yes/no questions (inversion).

Other common adverbs/adverbial phrases used in this way are: *not only, not till ..., nowhere, under no circumstances, in no way, rarely.*

(b) **Here comes** the bus. – **There goes** my train. – **In came** Tom Adams. – **Out went** the light. – **Up went** the prices again.

(But: Here it comes. – There it goes. – In he came. – etc.)

The adverbs *here, there, in, out, up, down, round, over, back* are often put at the beginning of short sentences in colloquial English. When the subject is a noun (not a pronoun) they're followed by inversion of the subject and verb. No auxiliary is used with this pattern.

4 Some more sentences with if-clauses

a "should" in the if-clause

Of course we'll let you know **if** we **should** change our decision.
Even **if** you **should** happen to be late, it doesn't matter.

Instead of the simple present, *should* + infinitive is possible in the if-clause. It's used when the action is thought to be unlikely. Compare:

If Pat rings up ... (i.e. I'm expecting a call from her.)
If Pat should ring up ... (i.e. I'm not expecting a call from her.)

b omission of "if" + inversion

If anything should go wrong, | call this number.
Should anything go wrong, |

If we'd known | what to expect, we certainly wouldn't have gone.
Had we known |

In if-clauses with *should* and *had* the *if* can be left out, but the clause must then begin with *should* or *had*.

4 (c) "will/would" in the if-clause

If you listen, you'll understand the story. (Wenn du zuhörst, ...)
If you'll just listen, I'll tell you about it. (Wenn du bitte mal zuhören möchtest, ...)
I'd be very grateful if you would check this for me.
If Jim won't help, we'll ask someone else.

As you know, *will* and *would* cannot normally be used in if-clauses. However, they can be used with the meaning "be willing to do something". In this way they are useful for polite requests, e.g.:

If you'll just wait here. – If you wouldn't mind coming with me.

Revision

5 Sentences with if-clauses

a If-clauses with the simple present/present progressive/present perfect

If you leave in five minutes, you'll be in time for the 6.30 train.⁺
                ... wirst du ... erreichen./... erreichst du ... .
If he isn't invited, John won't come.
If we want to make progress, we must work together.
If you don't like it here, go somewhere else.
If they're having trouble with the machine, they should ask an expert.
If you're driving to the airport, you can give Sally a lift.
If she's worked well, she ought to get a good mark.
If everybody has understood number one, we can go on to number two.
In the main clause: will-future/modal/imperative.
But when *if* means *whenever*, the simple present is used in both clauses.

If you drive fast, you use more petrol. – If water freezes, it becomes ice.

b If-clause with the past perfect

If I'd not been there myself, I'd never have believed it.
                ... hätte ich es nie geglaubt.
If we'd known about the plan earlier, we could have come too.
If the car hadn't had a breakdown, we might have arrived in time.
In the main clause: *would have/could have/might have*.
Note: in the if-clause *'d = had*, in the main clause *'d = would*.

c If-clause with the simple past

If I was ten years older, I wouldn't have to do any more "Klassenarbeiten".
                ... müßte ich keine Klassenarbeiten mehr schreiben.
If we had a car, we could drive there.
If you didn't listen to your teacher, what might happen?
In the main clause: *would/could/might*.

⁺ The main clause can also come at the beginning of the sentence of course:
You'll be in time for the 6.30 train if you leave in five minutes.

Unit 3 A

1. At 9.34 pm on July 13th, 1977 the lights went out in New York City and 9 million people were without electricity for up to 25 hours. Lightning had damaged several key cables, and the city's emergency system was unable to cope with the situation.
Subway trains stopped in their tunnels; people found themselves stuck in elevators; without their air-conditioning people really felt the hot and humid night. In the ghettos there was chaos: crowds in the streets shouted, "It's Christmas again!" and looted thousands of shops. Over 3500 people were arrested during the blackout. The next morning New Yorkers were shocked at the terrible things that had happened.

2. In many parts of the U.S. the winters of both 1977 and 1978 brought the worst weather in 200 years with snowstorms and strong winds that sent the temperature

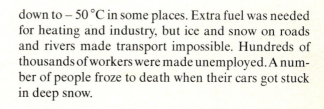

down to −50 °C in some places. Extra fuel was needed for heating and industry, but ice and snow on roads and rivers made transport impossible. Hundreds of thousands of workers were made unemployed. A number of people froze to death when their cars got stuck in deep snow.

3   Politics too can cause a crisis. In 1973, during the Arab-Israeli war, the Arab oil-producing countries refused to sell their oil to certain nations – including the U.S., Britain and West Germany. The result was that, for a time, petrol supplies became scarce. There were often long queues outside filling-stations. In West Germany no private motor traffic was allowed on Sundays during the crisis. After the Arab countries had lifted their embargo, they demanded huge increases in the price of oil. Before the embargo, the U.S. had paid between $3 and $4 for a barrel of imported oil. Afterwards, it cost between $12 and $13.

3 A

4 What happened to the Americans in 1973 can happen again. During such crises people suddenly become aware of their dependence on coal, gas, oil and other sources of energy. Consider your own life. How dependent are *you* on energy? Think especially of examples with electricity!

5 During the 1973 oil crisis a lot of people were forced to change their energy-consuming habits. For example, people who worked at the same place often got together to form car pools for their journeys to and from work. And new lower speed limits were introduced in all the countries hit by the embargo. But most of these measures were temporary; as soon as the crisis was over and the energy supply was back to normal, so were most people's habits (see diagram on right).

U.S. oil imports 1972-77
(in millions of barrels per day)

1972	1973	1974	1975	1976	1977
4·72	6·23	6·1	6·08	7·2	8·45

6 But then why should people's habits change anyway? Why should we be careful about our consumption of energy when there's no crisis? The answer is clear if you consider this fact: the consumption of energy in the world is rising while, at the same time, the reserves of coal, gas and oil in the world are falling. All experts agree that the reserves of these "fossil" fuels are exhaustible. One day they will run out. The only question is when. On this point the experts don't agree.
Firstly, for obvious practical reasons, it's difficult to know how much coal, gas or oil lies hidden below the surface in a particular field. Secondly, it's even more difficult to predict how many more deposits may still be discovered. Thirdly, it depends on whether alternative sources of energy can be developed. And finally, what makes any accurate forecast almost impossible is the fact that so much is dependent on political and economic developments throughout the world. Compare these two forecasts[1], made in 1976:

The known reserves of:	will last till:	
Oil	1997	2020
Gas	2004	2035
Coal	2080	2130

In 1977 James Schlesinger, U.S. President Carter's chief adviser on energy, estimated that the U.S.A. **has** enough coal for 400 years. Other experts predicted that the coal **will** last only 50-90 years.

[1] Quelle: Bundesanstalt für Geowissenschaften und Rohstoffe

ENERGY

Some background notes

Oil in its natural state – crude oil – must be refined <u>in order to</u> produce petrol, diesel oil, fuel oil for heating, as well as plastics and other chemical products.

<u>Apart from</u> being used for heating, coal is used to manufacture gas and coke, or to drive turbines that generate electricity.

Uranium is the raw material used to produce nuclear power (by fission), which is then <u>converted into electricity</u>. Scientists also hope they'll be able to <u>produce electricity</u> by nuclear fusion one day in the future.

Water, too, is a source of energy. Water power can be used to <u>drive turbines</u> to make electricity.

New words

crude oil
fuel oil
plastic
coke
turbine
uranium
fission
fusion
refine
manufacture
drive
generate
convert

Where does it come from? Where does it go to?

Some <u>comparative figures</u> for the U.S.A. and West Germany

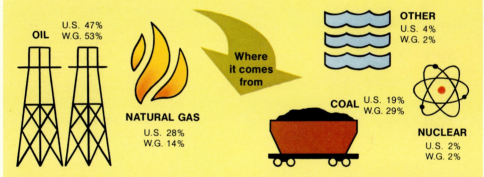

OIL U.S. 47% W.G. 53%

NATURAL GAS U.S. 28% W.G. 14%

Where it comes from

OTHER U.S. 4% W.G. 2%

COAL U.S. 19% W.G. 29%

NUCLEAR U.S. 2% W.G. 2%

c. 25% of the total is used by the energy industry itself (for refining crude oil, manufacturing gas and coke, etc.). The rest is consumed as follows:

INDUSTRIAL U.S. 38% W.G. 39%

Where it goes

HOUSEHOLD/ COMMERCIAL U.S. 35% W.G. 43%

TRANSPORT U.S. 27% W.G. 18%

3 A

7 Roughly speaking, as much energy has been consumed in the 20th century so far as in all the 19 centuries before that, and world consumption is increasing yearly. This is not due, however, to population growth. Not only is the total consumption increasing, so is the per capita consumption in most countries. In other words, each person consumes more energy each year, and this is true for developing nations as well as industrialized nations, as the figures in the table show.

Energy consumption per capita (in kilograms of coal equivalent)		
	1961	1975
India	151	221
Brazil	339	670
Japan	1300	3622
West Germany	3600	5345
Great Britain	4900	5265
United States	8000	10999

● One reason for the constant increase in energy consumption is that industry is using more and more machines. What other reasons can you think of?

8 On the one hand, we have rising consumption; on the other, non-renewable reserves. What can be done? What possibilities are there?

One possibility lies in the search for new deposits of coal, gas and oil (e.g. in Alaska, the North Sea). But from year to year it gets harder and more expensive, while the chances of success get less. Only one drilling in over a hundred leads to a profitable find. There are men who have spent **their lives** searching for oil without once making a really good find. Besides, even when oil or gas is found, it may not be worth exploiting. The cost of transporting the product to where it's needed as well as possible damage to the environment are important factors. The Alaska pipeline, for example, cost nearly $9 billion[1] to build, a large part of which was used for preventing damage to the environment.

An oil drilling rig in the North Sea

S 3a · Ex 5

● Even if more oil can be found and transported economically, there may be more urgent things to do with it than turn it into petrol, diesel or fuel oil. Crude oil is one of the basic raw materials in the chemical industry. What products are made from it? Find out as many as you can.

[1] billion (here: AE) a thousand millions; (BE) a million millions

9 Another possibility lies in developing alternative sources of energy. Nuclear power is one example everyone has heard about. However, so far, it is produced from a raw material – uranium – which is only found in certain countries and which, too, will one day run out. In addition there are, as you know, very great dangers involved in producing nuclear power.

Some alternative sources have always been with us and will never run out: the sun, the wind and the sea with its tides. Each has advantages and disadvantages **of its own**.

S 3b, 3c · Ex 7

Top left: Biblis nuclear power station, West Germany   Top right: a private house heated by solar power near Nürtingen, West Germany   Bottom left: a windmill in Sandusky, Ohio, U.S.A.   Bottom right: a tidal power station at St. Malo, France

3 A

10

energy source	advantages	disadvantages
nuclear power	+ no smoke; cheaper than coal; ...	– radioactive waste; problem of waste-disposal; problem of safety; ...
solar power	+ no pollution; ...	– expensive to install; not effective in all areas; ...
wind power	+ no pollution; ...	– difficult to store power; source unpredictable; ...
tidal power	+ no pollution; ...	– only possible in areas with very high tides; technological developments necessary; ...

● What other advantages/disadvantages can you think of for these energy sources? What other energy sources can you think of?

11 Finally we mustn't forget the obvious possibility, which is open to all of us: conservation of energy, i.e. being more efficient in our use of energy and avoiding unnecessary waste. Here's a short list of suggestions:
– better insulation of houses, offices, etc.
– recycling of used materials, e.g. aluminium, newspapers, bottles, etc.
– re-using warm water from industry to heat buildings
– making machines and vehicles more efficient (the average U.S. car in 1977 did 13.5 miles per gallon = 22 litres/100 km)

● Go on and add your suggestions.

12 A recent survey of U.S. teenagers showed that nearly all of them said they were concerned about energy, but that very few of them were actually doing anything about it. A similar result could, no doubt, be expected in West Germany. And it isn't difficult to understand why. We can't go out and drill for oil ourselves, nor can we all work at developing alternative sources of energy. Most people believe that it is far more important for governments and the huge multi-national companies to rethink their energy policies than for individual people to change their habits. This is obviously true, but the really important thing to remember is this: the plans for action suggested above must *all* be pursued together if we want to make sure that there will be enough energy in the future. **Everybody** must make **their** own contribution, whether big or small.

S 4 · Ex 6

OIL MAN

They drove down the M4 from Reading to Heathrow in Pete's new sports car. Marilyn always went to the airport with him, although it was not very easy for her to take time off work once a month.

Pete usually tried to act cheerful, at least until the plane took off, but this time he was too upset and angry. He hardly said a word to his girl-friend the whole journey. He had had an argument with his father the night before, and he could not get it out of his mind.

They sat in Terminal 1 Car Park, still not speaking, watching the autumn leaves falling from the trees. Marilyn's face, pale and tense, was almost hidden behind her long dark hair. It was time to go. "Bye, love. See you in two weeks." – "Bye, Pete. Be careful." He kissed her quickly, got out of the car, took his new suitcase from the boot, and walked over towards the terminal building. Marilyn saw him wave and disappear – but she did not leave at once. She sat there for nearly an hour, before driving slowly back to Reading.

✳

The flight to Aberdeen took an hour and a quarter. There, as usual, about 60 men were standing around in the crowded Helicopter Terminal Building, waiting to be flown out to their own particular oil rig in the North Sea. Alcohol was not allowed on the rigs, so some of the men were enjoying a last drink in the bar. Others were choosing a paperback novel to take with them. A plane from France landed. Pete looked at the passengers closely, hoping to spot Pierre, with whom he had shared a cabin last time. Then he remembered – Pierre had been transferred to an oil-field in the Persian Gulf.

✳

Pete's helicopter was full. 19 men were flying out with him. But he could not put names to all of their faces. Men were transferred from one rig to another so frequently that he had not got to know anyone really well, except perhaps Pierre. The noise of the engines made conversation more or less impossible and, as usual at the end of their two weeks ashore, everyone looked miserable. Only once, over a year ago now, on his first trip out to an oil rig, had Pete felt different. Then, he had been full of excitement.

During the 90-minute flight he kept thinking about the argument the previous night. His parents had always wanted him to take a steady job at the big ECA chemical factory near their house, where all kinds of plastic products were manufactured. Now, it seemed, there was a chance. Pete was a graduate in chemical engineering, and his father had heard that they would be advertising for somebody with his qualifications very soon. "Why don't you apply, son?" – "Look, Dad, there are a lot of unemployed graduates these

57

3 [T]

days, they might not give the job to me even if I did apply. But the thing is, ECA don't pay half as much as Interoil do." – "There's more to life than earning big money, son." – "Like what?" – "Well, if you ask me, you ought to make up your mind about Marilyn. Girls of her age want to get married – if not to you, then to someone else. You've been going out with her for three years now." – "That's my business, Dad, not yours!" –

Something bright appeared on the black sea below, and Pete watched as it became the painted reds, whites and yellows of the drilling rig. Nobody waved to welcome the men, as the helicopter landed on the platform 100 feet above the North Sea.

✳

He went down to the cabin he shared with three other men. Shifts were arranged so that two men in each cabin were asleep while the other two were working. Most of the personnel worked either from 12 o'clock in the morning to 12 o'clock at night or vice versa. But Pete had to work whenever it was necessary. Once he had had to work 24 hours non-stop. Slowly his nose got accustomed to the antiseptic smell in the air again. He put on his working clothes and hard shoes, put his "home clothes" in the grey aluminium cupboard, smiled sourly, and went along to the mud room. Throughout the sleeping-quarters the walls were covered with signs: 'Silence – Men Sleeping'. Outside, the signs said: 'No Smoking'.

Pete was a "mudman", a mud engineer. He was part of a team which controlled the mixture of mud pumped into the hole during drilling. His was a key job, as the chemicals stopped the bit from getting too hot, washed and cleaned the sides of the hole, and helped to prevent a sudden blow-out of oil or gas, the danger the oil men feared most. "Our rigs are 101% safe," the director of Interoil's Texas training centre had claimed. But Pete was aware that there had recently been a serious blow-out in a Norwegian field not far away. Thousands of tons of crude oil had poured into the North Sea, polluting the environment and turning the drilling platform into an unimaginable fire risk.

He found it difficult to concentrate throughout the first day. His father's words kept going round in his mind. But everyone in the team depended on the others working efficiently – not making a mistake. The sacks of mud chemicals had to be checked and re-ordered, to make sure that they did not run out; accurate instructions had to be given to the roustabouts, who then fetched the required chemicals from the next room and helped Pete to mix the right type of mud in big "mud pits"; and tests had to be done on the mud samples that were constantly being brought up the well-hole to the surface. Pete did not want to be responsible for anything going wrong. So he forced himself to concentrate. Gradually, he got back into the routine.

✳

3 [T]

At midnight he went to the dining-room. He took off his safety helmet, ordered a steak, took a plastic cup of milk and a piece of fresh apple pie, and sat down next to Chuck Vaughan, the large weathered tool pusher from Louisiana. In some ways Pete envied Chuck, who had worked on rigs and pipelines from Alaska to Saudi Arabia. Chuck shook his head. "Bloody milk!" After the meal Pete said, "By the way, Chuck, how did you like Alaska?" Chuck yawned. "Nice place." Then he went to join some other men for a game of cards.

Pete lay on his bunk and tried to sleep, but at first he was too exhausted, his mind too full of ideas. He smoked cigarette after cigarette, far more than he used to smoke – just as his consumption of beer seemed to rise every time he went ashore. He thought of Pierre and the Persian Gulf and the possibility of promotion. People were given responsibility fast in the oil industry.

The other man off duty in Pete's cabin was Wag McEldowney, a young engineer from New Zealand, who was already a drilling expert in spite of his age. "Didn't you say you'd worked in Nigeria, Wag?" – "Sure. Nice place." Pete was reminded of what Chuck had said about Alaska. It seemed it did not make much difference which country you were in, if all you saw was drilling equipment, an airport and a few hotel bars. What would he himself say, if someone asked him about the North Sea?

He remembered how he had driven to Heathrow. He was stupid. He ought to have apologized to Marilyn before he left. He missed her already and felt lonely. "Are you married, Wag?" – Wag was 26, two years older than Pete. "No. Used to be. Never again. Two divorces are enough for me." –

*

The never-changing routine on the rig got on the men's nerves. At first some of them had exchanged remarks about their last leave – where they had been, or what they had spent their wages on. But, after a few days on the rig together, there was nothing new to talk about. Pete was glad when the first week was over. There was no real weekend on the rig – they worked 7 days a week – but he knew that there were only 7 more days to go now.

After the training course in Texas, the personnel chief had said: "... you'll be involved in the energy business, the most important job in the world. Oil is the lifeblood of every industrialized society. It's our own future and the future of our children ..." And for a while Pete had seen himself as a kind of technological hero, bringing urgently-needed oil to a grateful nation. It was a long time since he had felt like that, though, especially as they had not discovered any oil in 12 months' drilling. Two men on the rig, both geologists, had spent their whole careers searching for oil without ever making a find worth exploiting. How could they stand it? Years of work for nothing?

Then there was a nasty incident, partly because everyone on the rig was either bored or nervous. One of the blow-out preventers above the surface had broken. It was not reacting to the pressure of the mud properly and had to be replaced at once. Otherwise, if they hit oil or gas, there could be a blow-out. Pete was on the drilling deck talking to the crane driver. Suddenly Pietro, one of the Italian roustabouts, misunderstood an order. Bruce, a big hard-featured roughneck from Texas, exploded: "You bloody wop! Why don't you listen?" When Pietro shouted something back at him in Italian, Bruce hit him. A fight started, Pete moved in to separate the two men – and got a fist in his eye. He would have loved to fight back, but forced himself to calm down. It was Chuck, the tool pusher, who put an end to the matter. He rushed across when he heard the noise and pulled the two men apart.

*

Finally, it was the shift-change-day. Only a few more hours of loneliness and the helicopter would be taking him back to Aberdeen. As dawn came, he thought of Marilyn and the present he had planned for her. It was her birthday the following night and she was having a party. He was really looking forward to seeing her. His father was right. He ought to decide about Marilyn soon. She had mentioned the future several times during his last leave. One thing was sure, though, he was certainly not going to work for ECA!

3 T

The weather was getting worse. The temperature was only 3 °C. Heavy clouds formed over the rough black sea in the west. The wind screamed round the rig, the air was filled with spray. By mid-morning the clouds had become so dark it was difficult to see. Pete watched the mountains of black water rising and falling. He saw a huge wave reaching up towards the platform and felt a moment of panic.

A strong freezing rain began, the wind grew stronger, lightning lit the sky, and by noon 70-foot-high waves were almost reaching the drilling deck. Work had to stop and everyone knew that no helicopter or boat could reach the rig until the storm was over. The men were not concerned about their supplies running out but, if anyone became ill, they could not be taken ashore. They were prisoners.

Pete thought about Marilyn's birthday party and the low-paid lab-job at ECA. How long would he go on being an oil man?

- 1. Describe Pete's feelings at Heathrow airport. Then say why you think Marilyn stays there for almost an hour before driving slowly back.
  2. Pete's first shift begins as soon as he arrives. What advantages can you see in this arrangement? Why is the first shift always the worst?
  3. What details of work on an oil rig does the story give? Compare the positive and negative points. In what ways is the job dangerous?
  4. Do you think people work on oil rigs mainly because of the "excitement" (page 57, line 30) and the importance of "the energy business" (page 60, line 39) or because of other factors? Give reasons.
  5. What sort of personal problems can there be for people who work on oil rigs? What are the particular problems in Pete's case?
  6. Describe any changes you see in Pete's feelings during the story. Do you think he will join ECA after all? Quote from the text to support your view.
  7. In what way(s) is work on an oil rig different from most other jobs? What other jobs are roughly similar?
  8. Would you yourself like to work on an oil rig? Give reasons for your answer.

3 Ex

1 *The President of the United States is in London for a meeting of world leaders on the economic situation in developing countries and energy problems. A reporter is interviewing the President.*

Reporter: Mr President, what do you hope this meeting will achieve?
President: Well, the U.S.A. is a rich country, and we would like to help the poorer countries of this world more effectively. The meeting is going to study ways of helping developing countries to achieve greater economic progress.
Reporter: How much money does the U.S.A. give to developing countries?
President: We've always given generous help to developing countries. We gave 4 billion dollars last year, and it'll be even more this year.
Reporter: What about the trade situation?
President: Our trade with developing countries is growing, but the meeting ought to find a way of stopping sudden changes in the price of raw materials. This is what the developing countries want, and it's what I was discussing with the Zambian Prime Minister in Washington during his recent visit.
Reporter: Now, let's turn to energy. What do you hope to achieve here?
President: We should at least try to agree on a number of key issues.
Reporter: And they are?
President: Well, United States oil consumption is still too high and if nothing is done, it might get even higher. We want to reduce oil imports in particular.
Reporter: And what plans do you have for doing this?
President: Well, I wouldn't like to give details now.
Reporter: Thank you, Mr President.

Write the report of the interview in the next day's newspaper.

U.S. PRESIDENT ARRIVES IN LONDON FOR TALKS

The U.S. President arrived in London yesterday for a meeting of world leaders on energy and the economic situation in developing countries. He said the U.S.A. was a rich country and .... The meeting ..., he said. The President pointed out that the U.S.A. ... generous help to developing countries.

Go on.

Rev.

63

3 Ex

2 *The management of a car company are having a meeting. They're discussing the company's problems. Imagine you're the secretary and you have to write down the main points (in italics).*
Use these verbs: advise, agree, apologize, ask (2 ×), explain, invite, point out, promise, suggest (3 ×).

Mr Barlow:	... *so you see, we're losing money* because we're not selling enough cars.
Mr Sfortz:	*Why don't we reduce the number of workers?* We could save money if we had less wages to pay.
Mr Murray:	That'd mean trouble with the unions, wouldn't it?
Mr Barlow:	But we need to discuss the situation with the unions anyway. *Could you arrange a meeting with them next week, Mr Murray?*
Mr Holliday:	I say we should try to improve our sales. *What about a big sales campaign?* It's no good expecting to sell cars if we don't advertise.
Mr Murray:	*If I were you, I'd have another look at the company's financial position, Mr Holliday.* You'll see we haven't got enough money for an expensive campaign.
Mr Barlow:	When will you have the September sales figures, Mr Price?
Mr Price:	Oh, yes, the sales figures. *I'm sorry that they're rather late.* I should have them next Tuesday.
Mr Barlow:	Well, can you let me see them as soon as possible, please?
Mr Price:	*I'll give everyone a copy of the figures as soon as I have them.*
Mrs Shaw:	I think we could easily sell more cars if only we produced them. *Let's for heaven's sake try to produce more cars.* A lot of garages say they can sell our cars, but they can never get enough of them.
Mr Davidson:	Right. The problem is producing the cars, not selling them.
Mr Barlow:	Well, *we're going to discuss this problem with Mr Cohen next week.* – But before we finish, here's something a little more pleasant. *Would everyone like to come to a party at my house on Saturday the 26th?*

Mr Barlow explained that they were losing money.
Mr Sfortz ... reducing the number of workers.
Mr Barlow ... .

Go on.

Rev.

3   One Saturday afternoon Barbara Dixon had to stay at home to look after her younger sister. She decided to phone a few friends and chat to them. Here are some of the things she said:

It's three days later. Report what Barbara said to her friends.

1. Barbara told Sue that she believed Pat ... .
2. She asked Chris whether ... .   *Go on.*

Rev.

4 Paragraph writing

Write down and complete the following table:

	advantages	disadvantages
walking	+ helps to keep you fit + costs nothing + saves fuel	– slow – only short journeys possible – inconvenient in bad weather
bike	+ ...	– ...
car	+ ...	– ...
train	+ ...	– ...
plane	+ ...	– ...

Now write a paragraph about one *of the ways of travelling. Example:*

The advantages of walking are that it helps to keep you fit, and that it costs nothing because you do not have to buy fuel (except of course the food you eat to give you the energy to walk). It helps to save our reserves of energy if people walk instead of going by car. The disadvantages are that it takes a long time to walk more than a few miles, and walking is not very nice in bad weather.

3 Ex

5 Here's a news item from a South Wales newspaper. Fill in a possessive adjective and these nouns: anorak, arm, balance, leg, life, lunch, mind, voice, way, wife. Some of the nouns must be put in the plural.

Man breaks Leg in Black Mountains

28-year-old Barry Townsend of Huddersfield, West Yorkshire, was brought down from the Black Mountains yesterday with a broken leg. He was taken to hospital in Pontypool, where he is said to be comfortable. Mr Townsend was on a walking holiday with *his wife* Cathy and another man, Mr Graham Spooner, also of Huddersfield. Mr Townsend has lost ... and can only whisper a few words, so his wife told us the story. "We ate ... at about twelve," Mrs Townsend said, "but soon afterwards we must have taken the wrong path because we lost ... . Then it started to rain, too, so we made up ... to go back. We were walking down a steep path when Barry lost ... and fell about twenty feet. When we found he'd broken ..., Graham went to get help. Barry and I both felt cold and ... were getting wet. I held him and put ... round him to keep him warm. Help came in about three hours. We were lucky. We're very grateful to everyone. They saved ... ."

6 Some of the rules at an English school might be written like this:

```
1. Every pupil is to be in his classroom by 9 am.
2. If a pupil is late, he should apologize to his
   teacher.
3. No pupil is allowed to leave school before 4 pm
   without his teacher's permission.
4. If a pupil goes home to lunch, he is expected
   to return by 1.30 pm.
5. Every pupil should do his homework before 9 pm.
6. A pupil who wishes can do his homework at school
   between 4 pm and 6 pm.
7. No pupil is permitted to spend his lunch break
   inside the school building.
8. Every pupil is to wear his uniform on school days.
9. If a pupil behaves badly, he is given extra work
   by his form teacher.
```

Now make the rules sound a little less formal by using "everybody", "anybody" and "nobody".

1. Everybody is to be in their classroom by 9 o'clock.
2. If anybody is late, they should apologize to ... teacher.
3. Nobody is allowed to leave school ... .

Go on.

7 *Replace the phrases in italics by e.g. "a room of your own", "a habit of hers", "some records of John's".*

Liz: Well, this is my room.
Val: It's nice. You're lucky to have *your own room*. I have to share with my sister. And talking in her sleep is *one of her habits*, unfortunately.
Liz: Let's play some music, shall we? There are still *a few of my brother's records* here.
Val: He lets you borrow them then?
Liz: Yes, because he uses my record-player – he hasn't got *his own record-player*.
Val: Have you got any Don Weston records? He's *one of my great favourites*.
Liz: I like him, too. I think he's got *his own style*. Yes, here's "I Can't Forget You".
Val: I like *his other hit* – what was it?
Liz: "Broken Heart". – I quite like the Crying Five. Do you?
Val: Not a lot. But Steve Patterson is *one of their fans*. Do you know him?
Liz: Yes, Steve's *one of my friends*. And his parents are *my parents' friends*.
Val: Doesn't he sing in a pop group?
Liz: That's right. I sang for them once, too, when *one of my boy-friends* was in the group.
Val: I wish I could sing. I like trying to write songs but I can't sing.
Liz: Well, I can't write songs.
Val: It's *one of my hobbies*.
Liz: We ought to get together. We'd make a great team.

8 **Vocabulary**

Choose the correct answer and make another sentence using the alternative.

Example: Before oil can be used, it must be a) refined b) manufactured.

Answer: a) Before oil can be used, it must be refined. Products can be manufactured from it.

1. Coal and oil are a) exhaustible b) inexhaustible sources of energy.
2. Oil in its natural state is called a) fuel oil b) crude oil.
3. Oil is sold a) by the ton b) by the barrel.
4. One kind of coal is a) coke b) petrol.
5. Coal and water can be used to drive a) windmills b) turbines.
6. Uranium is used to produce a) tidal power b) nuclear power.
7. Oil can be transported by a) pipeline b) cable.
8. Solar energy is energy from a) the sea b) the sun.
9. Conservation means a) not using all our reserves b) high consumption of energy.
10. Heating costs can be reduced by a) recycling b) insulation.

3 Ex

9 Present perfect – simple past

The Prime Minister, the leader of the Freedom Party, is talking on television a week before the general election.

Prime Minister:

Good evening. I just want to tell you what this government *has done* for you in the last few years.	do
When the Freedom Party ... to power five	come
years ago, this country ... in a mess, but	be
now the mistakes made by the Social	
Party ... right. The last government, if you	put (passive)
remember, ... all its promises. They ...	break, say
everything would be fine, but it wasn't.	
They ... prices go up too fast. Under the	let
last government the economy ... adequate	not give (passive)
attention, but under this government the	
standard of living ... and prices ... up so	improve, not go
quickly. This Freedom Party government	
... everything it promised. Last month the	do
number of people unemployed ... again	fall
by 30,000, in fact the number ... every	fall
month so far this year. And don't forget	
the old people. We ... old age pensioners	give
more money last year as we had promised.	
The Freedom Party ... what it has	always do
promised to do, but the Social Party ... its	always break
promises ever since it first ... to power.	come
Do you remember when they once ... they	say
would bring taxes down? Well, the	
Social Party ... taxes – ever; they	never reduce
... them up instead. Taxes ... up three	always put, go
times when they ... last in power.	be
The Freedom Party, on the other hand, ...	just reduce
taxes for the second time in three years.	
So I'm asking you to vote for the Freedom	
Party candidate in your constituency in	
next week's general election.	

Rev.

Interpreting

Eva Bruckmeier and three of her friends from Siegen are on a visit to Leeds, Siegen's twin town. They're sitting in a café, talking to some English teenagers about problems with their parents. As Eva can speak both German and English fairly fluently, she's acting as the group's interpreter.
Take Eva's part. Use all the interpreting techniques you've practised.

Andy: If you ask me, there's no question about it. My parents have got no say in the matter anyway. It's up to me what I wear, not them.
Eva: Andy meint, daß es allein seine Sache ist, ...
Ute: Er hat ganz recht. Völlig meine Meinung.
Eva: Ute ... .
Anne: Same with me. But I'm not so sure about what Hans was saying a few minutes ago – about friends. As far as I'm concerned, it's only fair to tell your parents who you're going out with.
Eva: ...
Hans: Na ja, sicher. Solange sie nur Bescheid wissen wollen, ist es ja in Ordnung. Aber wie sieht's aus, wenn sie Einwände machen? Du läßt dich davon doch sicher nicht beeinflussen, selbst wenn's Krach geben sollte, oder? Dann finde ich es beinahe besser, du gehst gar nicht erst auf Fragen ein, mit wem du verkehrst und so.
Eva: ...
Tony: I think Hans is right. In any case, what right have they got to know everything? We're not babies any more, are we?
Eva: ...
Irene: Das kannst du wohl laut sagen. Aber 'mal was anderes. Stell' dir vor, du willst gerade weg, irgendwohin. Da fragt dich dein Vater, was du vorhast. Mit vielen Zusatzfragen. Du hast es eilig, wirst ungeduldig. Dafür wird er immer redseliger. Du mußt dir unweigerlich eine uralte Story aus seiner Jugend anhören. Du bist sauer, er ist sauer. Dann gehst du trotzdem weg. Aber vielleicht wäre der ganze Ärger zu vermeiden gewesen, wenn du gleich beim Frühstück erwähnt hättest, was du vorhast.
Eva: ...
Andy: I don't know. Eva, ask Irene about pocket money, will you? Does she get the same amount every week, whether she's been a "good girl" or not?
Eva: ...

Go on with this conversation in class. Choose an interpreter and decide which pupils are to express their ideas in English, which in German. You might want to discuss topics such as: TV, hair-style, music, cigarettes, beer, Hausaufgaben, Eigenverantwortung, Abhängigkeit, Elternpflicht.

3 Ex

Communication practice: *Making requests and responding to them*

1   Here are some phrases you can use when making a request, together with some suggestions for positive and negative responses. As you already know from other exercises, some of the phrases are more polite than others:

> Will/Can you ..., please?
>   – Sure./Sorry, I'm afraid not.
> Would/Could you ..., please?
>   – Certainly./I'd love to, but ...
> Can/May I ..., please?
>   – Of course. Any time./Well, if you don't mind ...
> Is it okay/Would it be all right with you if I/he/they ...?
>   – Go ahead./Well, actually, I'd rather you didn't.
> Would you mind ...ing/if ...?
>   – Not at all./That's rather a lot to ask, don't you think?
> Could you do me a favour and ...?
>   – I'd be glad to./Well, I'm rather busy just at the moment.
> I'd appreciate it very much if ...
>   – That's all right with me./That's out of the question, I'm afraid.
> I wonder if it would be at all possible (for me/you/him, etc.) to ...?
>   – With pleasure. You're welcome to./I wish I could help, but ...

2   Here are two examples of short dialogues:

a) At a party

   Guest: Would you mind if I used your phone to call a taxi?
   Host: Not at all, you're welcome to. But I'm sure someone could give you a lift.

b) A student is talking to the owner of the block of flats where he lives.

   Student: I'd appreciate it very much if you could wait another month for the rent for June.
   Flat owner: Sorry, but that's out of the question I'm afraid.

3   Now fill in the missing parts of the following dialogues:

a) *Tommy:*   Dad, ... let me have the car Friday evening? Ellen and I have got tickets for the theatre.
   Mr Green: *(positive response)* ..., if you promise to drive carefully.

Communication practice

b) At the station Susan asks a stranger to help her with her two heavy suitcases.

Susan: ... lift these suitcases onto the train, please?
Stranger: (positive response) ...

c) Jack wants to borrow some money from his friend Eddie.

Jack: ... lend me £20? My motor-bike is being repaired and I haven't got enough money to pay the bill.
Eddie: (negative response) ... It took you six months to pay me back the last time.

4 Now use the following situations to make up similar dialogues in which people make requests and respond to them. You may choose positive or negative responses:

a) Mr Ferguson's car won't start. He asks a neighbour to help him to push it.
b) Mrs Barton asks the people in the flat next to hers to turn down their TV.
c) Pauline asks a classmate to shut the window because she's cold.
d) Caroline asks the French teacher not to give the class any homework for the next day, because there's a party at school that evening.
e) Al is having trouble with his TV set. He asks his friend George, who works at a radio and TV shop, to have a look at it.
f) Mrs Johnson asks her husband to do the shopping, because she's busy washing the curtains.
g) Mr O'Brian asks his son Jeff to wash the car.
h) Mr Bancroft is queuing for a ticket at the station. He asks the people in front of him if he can move up in the queue because his train leaves in three minutes.
i) Richard asks his parents if he can give a party for his friends.
j) At the dinner table Steve asks the hostess whether she minds if he smokes.
k) It's a beautiful spring afternoon and several pupils ask their teacher whether they can have their English lesson outside on the school playing-field.
l) Mr Davis asks his boss whether he can go home early on Wednesday afternoon to watch an important cricket match on TV.

3 [S]

1 Revision: Reported speech

a with a change of tense

Colin: "I **love** Cindy." – Colin said (that) he **loved** Cindy.
Karen: "What **have** you **got** for me?" – Karen asked what I **had** for her.
Tina: "I **came** at 6. I **haven't been** here long."
Tina pointed out that she**'d come** at 6 and so **hadn't been** there long.
Steve: "**I'll help** you if I **can**, Susie."
Steve promised Susie that he**'d help** her if he **could**.
Ed: "**Were** you **watching** TV when the phone **rang**?"
Ed asked us if/whether we**'d been watching** TV when the phone **had rung**.

b with no change of tense

Mary: "**I'd like to** go with Alan, but I think he **might** be busy."
Mary said she**'d like to** go with Alan, but she thought he **might** be busy.
Tony: "You really **ought to** visit Leeds – I **used to** live there."
Tony told us we really **ought to** visit Leeds – he **used to** live there.
Jean: "What **should** I wear to Howard's party, I wonder?"
Jean wondered what she **should** wear to Howard's party.

Might, ought to, should, used to and *would like to* don't change in reported speech.

c Reported commands, invitations, requests, suggestions and advice

Commands:

Al: "Don't wait for Pat, go straight in."
Al **told us not to** wait for Pat but **to** go straight in.
Or: Al told us we **weren't to** wait for Pat, we **were to** go straight in.

Invitations:

Jack: "Will/Won't you join us after the party, Marcia?"
Jack **invited** Marcia **to** join them after the party.

Requests:

Lynn: "Can/Could/Will/Would you turn the radio down, please, Tom?"
Lynn **asked** Tom **to** turn the radio down.

Suggestions:

Arthur: "Shall we get the expensive tickets?"
Rachel: "No, let's get the cheap ones."
Arthur **suggested** get**ting** the expensive tickets but Rachel disagreed. She **suggested that** they **should** get the cheap ones.

Advice:
Mother: "If I were you, Jane, I'd take the exam."
Her mother **advised** Jane **to** take the exam.

The choice of the reporting verb is important as it shows the speaker's intention.
In addition to the ones used above, there are many more verbs which are suitable for other contexts, e.g. *complain, apologize, promise, grumble, remark, warn, be sure, explain, declare,* etc.

d Changes in adverbial expressions of place and time

Bob (to Sue outside the station on Monday morning): "Lynn had an accident **here yesterday**. Did you know?"
Sue (to Mary at school later that day): "Bob told me Lynn had had an accident **outside the station yesterday**."
Sue (to Jill in town the next day): "I met Bob outside the station yesterday and he told me Lynn had had an accident **there on Sunday**."
Jane (to Alan outside the station some days later): "I was talking to Bob on Monday and he told me Lynn had had an accident **here the day before**."

Adverbial expressions of place and time in direct speech must sometimes be changed when they're reported. The changes depend on the time and place of the reporting. The following changes are often necessary with time expressions:

today	→ that day
yesterday	→ the day before
tomorrow	→ the next/following day
next week	→ the following week/a week later
last month	→ the previous month/a month before

(2) More about reported speech

When direct speech is reported, there's usually a change of tense (present → past, past → past perfect, etc.). However, a tense change isn't always necessary.

(a) No tense change with introducing verb in present/present perfect/future

Jim: "My favourite dessert **is** ice-cream with chocolate sauce."
Jim **says** his favourite dessert **is** ice-cream with chocolate sauce.
Jim **has** always **said** his favourite dessert **is** ice-cream with chocolate sauce.
If you ask Jim, he**'ll tell** you his favourite dessert **is** ice-cream with chocolate sauce.

3 [S]

(b) No tense change when statement is still true

Tom: "Pigs **can't** fly."
Tom said pigs **can't** fly.
Sue: "What **do** you do in your spare time, John?"
Sue wanted to know what I **do** in my spare time.

The tense needn't be changed if the statement is true at any time (Pigs can't ever fly.), or if it's still correct at the time when reported (What John does in his spare time hasn't changed meanwhile.).

(c) No change of simple past/past progressive

Ross: "I **was** late yesterday."
Ross pointed out that he**'d been**/he **was** late the day before.
Bob: "Tim **arrived** while I **was having** a bath."
Bob remarked that Tim **had arrived**/Tim **arrived** while he **was having** a bath.

In written English the simple past is usually changed to the past perfect (the past progressive to the past perfect progressive) in reported speech; in spoken English there's often no change of these tenses.

(d) Change or no change with must/needn't/mustn't

Sally: "I really **must** finish the work soon."
Sally said she really **had to** finish the work soon.

Must/needn't are usually changed to *had to/didn't have to*. But:

1. *Sue:* "Someone at the door? Oh, it **must** be Ed."
   Sue thought it **must** be Ed at the door. } a deduction

   "We really **must** meet again soon."
   She said they really **must** meet again soon. } a suggestion

   "You simply **must** see Pollini's new film."
   She told me I simply **must** see Pollini's new film. } advice

   When used like this, *must* doesn't usually change in reported speech.

2. *Bob:* "I **must** ring Al up if he doesn't write soon."
   Bob said he**'d have to** ring Al up if he didn't write soon.

   Must/needn't are changed to *would(n't) have to* in reported speech when they refer to the future, i.e. when they mean *will/won't have to*.

3. *Linda:* "You **mustn't** talk like that about your sister."
   Linda said I **mustn't**/**wasn't to** talk like that about my sister.

   Mustn't either stays the same or can be changed to *wasn't/weren't to*.

3 More about possessives

a Possessive adjectives (for German definite article)

Brian broke **his leg** skiing. (...sich das Bein...)
I washed **my hair** last night. (...mir die Haare...)
The boys had **their hands** in **their pockets**. (...die Hände in den Taschen.)
The quick action of the firemen saved **our lives**. (...uns das Leben.)

The possessive adjective – not the definite article – is used with parts of the body, clothes and a few other nouns very closely linked with human beings (e.g. *life, death*). In English these nouns are usually plural where more than one person is concerned, in German the singular is used:

Their action saved our live**s**. (...uns das Leben.)
The guests put on their hat**s** and coat**s**. (...Hut und Mantel...)

b of mine, of yours, of hers, of Peter's, etc.

Lynn has always been a friend **of mine**. (...eine Freundin von mir.)
Please tell Bob I'm sorry, I've still got three records **of his**.
It's a habit **of Christine's** to go to the hairdresser's every week.

Remember: *of* + possessive (never personal pronoun, as in German).

c of my own, etc.

I have my own room. Have you a room **of your own**? (...ein eigenes Zimmer?)

Before a noun, *own* is never used with the indefinite article.

4 Concord with somebody, anybody, nobody, everybody

Oh look, **somebody** has left his/**their** gloves on this seat.
If **anybody** wants to help, he/**they** should say so now.
Nobody is interested in such an old camera, is he/are **they**?
Everybody agrees with the idea, don't **they**?

Although the indefinite pronouns *somebody/someone, anybody/anyone, nobody/no-one* are always followed by a singular verb, they're often followed – especially in colloquial English – by the plural forms *their, they* and *them*. *Everybody/everyone* are nearly always followed by *their, they* and *them*.

Unit 4 A/T

This Unit contains a number of poems and narrative texts by British and American writers.

Most of them can, of course, be simply read and enjoyed without any help or background information. However, to fully appreciate a piece of literature and get the maximum enjoyment out of it, it is advisable to read it closely and critically, more thoroughly than you would read, for example, certain sections of a daily paper.

What is more, there are a number of techniques which can be learned and which will help the reader to get the most out of any poem or work of fiction. Some aids to appreciation have been summarized in two special sections (on this page and on page 87). They should be referred to when dealing with the questions following the poems and narrative texts.

Talking about poetry

Poems are often divided into *verses* (also called *stanzas*).
Robert Frost's poem consists of four verses, each of four *lines*.

The *rhyme scheme* of the first verse is a a b a.

The pattern produced by stressed and unstressed syllables is known as *metre*. One unit of stressed and unstressed syllables is called a *foot*.
The lines of Frost's poem, for example, have four feet:

> x / | x / | x / | x /
> But I have pro mises to keep.

When you read this line aloud, however, you will see that its *rhythm* does not correspond to the metre because some syllables are stressed differently. You might, for example, read it like this:

> But 'I have 'promises to 'keep.

When talking about a poem, it may be helpful to consider the following points. For example, what is the poet talking about? What is the *subject matter* or *theme* of the poem? Does it take place anywhere? Is there a particular *setting*? Is a particular *atmosphere* created?

What's the *tone* of the poem, i.e. the poet's attitude towards the reader? Is it serious or playful, formal or informal, or perhaps ironic?

Poets often like to express things in a more effective, individual way, e.g. by using *images*. Instead of simply saying that somebody is strong, a poet might use a *simile*: "He was as strong as a horse." or a *metaphor*: "He was a tower of strength."

Certain words, besides their actual meaning, can have additional *connotations* for the reader. For example, the word "home" means the place where somebody lives, but for a particular reader it may have connotations of being happy/unhappy, secure/insecure, etc. Writers frequently choose words knowing, or hoping, that they will have particular connotations for the reader.

4 A/T

Stopping by woods on a snowy evening[+]

Whose woods these are I think I know.
His house is in the village though;
He will not see me stopping here
To watch his woods fill up with snow.

My little horse must think it queer
To stop without a farmhouse near
Between the woods and frozen lake
The darkest evening of the year.

He gives his harness bells a shake
To ask if there is some mistake.
The only other sound's the sweep
Of easy wind and downy flake.

The woods are lovely, dark and deep,
But I have promises to keep,
And miles to go before I sleep,
And miles to go before I sleep.

Robert Frost

- 1. Analyse a) the metre and rhythm, b) the rhyme scheme. What effect is produced by them? Is it the same effect?
  2. How would you describe the atmosphere of the poem? The sound of some words can help in creating an atmosphere. Can you find examples of words which the poet might have chosen for this reason?
  3. What connotations – if any – do the words "snow" and "sleep" have for you?
  4. The last line repeats the line before. What effect does this have? Do you think the two lines should be spoken in the same way when read aloud?
  5. Having read the poem several times, what can you say about its subject matter and its setting?
  6. What do we learn about the feelings of the speaker ("I")? We're not really told why he interrupts his journey, but which line comes closest to giving the reason in your opinion?
  *7. Some people see a symbolic meaning in Frost's poem. They interpret the snow-filled woods as a symbol for the power of beauty or death. Comment on this interpretation. Can you suggest any other interpretation?
  8. Even after repeated reading, the poem leaves a number of questions open. What questions do you ask yourself on reading it?
  *9. It has been said that a poem is created not by the poet alone, but also by the reader. Try and explain this, using Frost's poem as your example.

[+] The new words from the poems and narrative texts can be found on pages 145-147. Some notes about the authors appear on page 118.

4 A/T

The Icingbus

the littleman
with the hunchbackedback
creptto his feet
to offer his seat
to the blindlady

people gettingoff
steered carefully around
the black mound
of his back
as they would a pregnantbelly

the littleman
completely unaware
of the embarrassment behind
watched as the blindlady
fingered out her fare

. . . . . .

muchlove later he suggested that instead
ofa wedding-cake they shouldhave a miniaturebus
made outof icing but she laughed
andsaid that buses werefor travelling in
and notfor eating and besides
you cant taste shapes.

Roger McGough

- 1. How does the poet refer to the two characters in the poem? Why doesn't he mention their names?
  2. What two moments of their lives are mentioned? Why only these?
  3. The six dots between verses 3 and 4 are a part of the poem. Why?
  4. Why do you suppose the man wants to have a bus made out of icing instead of an ordinary wedding-cake? Try to explain the woman's reaction to this suggestion.
  5. Analyse the rhyme scheme and the rhythm of the poem. Can you see any purpose for the change in the last verse?
  *6. Many words are written in a non-standard way. What reasons can you imagine the poet had for doing this?
  *7. The effect of the poem is very much dependent on its tone. Try to describe the tone in which it's written.

Pantomime Poem

"HE'S BEHIND YER!"
chorused the children
but the warning came too late.

The monster leaped forward
and fastening its teeth into his neck,
tore off the head.

The body fell to the floor
"MORE" cried the children
"MORE, MORE, MORE

MORE

MOF

Roger McGough

- 1. The first thing that strikes the reader about this poem is its unusual printed form. Describe this form and try to say what its function is.
- 2. Compare the children's attitude to the monster at the beginning of the poem and at the end. Comment on this.

4 A/T

```
l(a

le
af
fa

ll

s)
one
l

iness
```

e. e. cummings

- This poem can't be read in the normal way. But, if you look carefully, you can read the part which is inside the brackets and you can read the part outside the brackets.
  1. Consider the part inside the brackets. What connotations do these words have for you?
  2. The three words in the brackets are put inside another word. What is achieved by this unusual arrangement?
  *3. The division of the words and the arrangement of the letters are also unusual. What effect do you think the poet intended to produce by this? (Think of the image created by the words in the brackets.)

4

Tonight at noon

Tonight at noon
Supermarkets will advertise 3p EXTRA on everything
Tonight at noon
Children from happy families will be sent to live in a home
Elephants will tell each other human jokes
America will declare peace on Russia
World War I generals will sell poppies in the streets on November 11th
The first daffodils of autumn will appear
When the leaves fall upwards to the trees

Tonight at noon
Pigeons will hunt cats through city backyards
Hitler will tell us to fight on the beaches and on the landing fields
A tunnel full of water will be built under Liverpool
Pigs will be sighted flying in formation over Woolton
and Nelson will not only get his eye back but his arm as well
White Americans will demonstrate for equal rights
in front of the Black House
and the Monster has just created Dr Frankenstein

Girls in bikinis are moonbathing
Folksongs are being sung by real folk
Artgalleries are closed to people over 21
Poets get their poems in the Top 20
Politicians are elected to insane asylums
There's jobs for everyone and nobody wants them
In back alleys everywhere teenage lovers are kissing
in broad daylight
In forgotten graveyards everywhere the dead will quietly
bury the living
and
You will tell me you love me
Tonight at noon

Adrian Henri

- Henri has written a poem full of paradoxical statements. What do you think his aim was in doing this?

Two Views of Leisure

Leisure

What is this life if, full of care,
We have no time to stand and stare.

No time to stand beneath the boughs
And stare as long as sheep or cows.

No time to see, when woods we pass,
Where squirrels hide their nuts in grass.

No time to see, in broad daylight,
Streams full of stars like skies at night.

No time to turn at Beauty's glance,
And watch her feet, how they can dance.

No time to wait till her mouth can
Enrich that smile her eyes began.

A poor life this if, full of care,
We have no time to stand and stare.

W. H. Davies

- 1. Describe the rhyme scheme of this poem. What is its effect?
- 2. Does the rhythm correspond to the subject matter?
- 3. What's your opinion of the images chosen by Davies to support his statement in the first verse?
- 4. How would you describe the tone of the poem?

Viewing Time

What is this life if, freed from care,
We have no time – except to stare.

No time to savour food and drink,
Or read, or write, or sit and think.

No time to paint, or play the flute,
Or dig, or yarn, or bottle fruit.

No time for politics, or pubs,
Discussion groups, or drama clubs.

No time for charity, or church,
Or local history research.

No time to give the dog a walk,
Or *play* a parlour game, or talk …

A poor life this, if we can spare
No time – except to sit and stare.

                    E. V. Milner

- 1. What's the subject matter of this poem? Apart from the title, there's one other key word. With what particular meaning is it used?
  2. Compare "Leisure" and "Viewing Time" from the point of view of form, subject matter and tone. Where are they similar/dissimilar?
  3. Milner's poem is an example of a parody. Its aim is to amuse by imitating the form, style or language of another work but changing the content and tone. Is Milner's poem to be understood only as a parody of Davies' poem, or do you think it could be read and appreciated on its own?

The Little Girl and the Wolf

One afternoon a big wolf waited in a dark forest for a little girl to come along carrying a basket of food to her grandmother. Finally a little girl did come along and she was carrying a basket of food. "Are you carrying that basket to your grandmother?" asked the wolf. The little girl said yes, she was. So the wolf asked her where her grandmother lived and the little girl told him and he disappeared into the wood.

When the little girl opened the door of her grandmother's house she saw that there was somebody in bed with a nightcap and nightgown on. She had approached no nearer than twenty-five feet from the bed when she saw that it was not her grandmother but the wolf, for even in a nightcap a wolf does not look any more like your grandmother than the Metro-Goldwyn lion[1] looks like Calvin Coolidge[2]. So the little girl took an automatic out of her basket and shot the wolf dead.

Moral: It is not so easy to fool little girls nowadays as it used to be.

James Thurber

[1] The lion that appears at the beginning of films made by Metro-Goldwyn-Mayer (MGM)
[2] U.S. President 1923-1929

4 A/T

- 1. Within the few lines of this text Thurber manages to amuse the reader. How? To answer this question, you need to think back to a famous fairy-story, whose English title is "Little Red Riding Hood". What differences can you see between "The Little Girl and the Wolf" and "Little Red Riding Hood"?
  2. The comic effect is achieved not only by the action, but also by Thurber's use of language. Which sentences do you find funny? Try to give reasons.
  3. "The Little Girl and the Wolf" is taken from Thurber's book "Fables for Our Time" (1943). What elements of a fable do you recognize here?
  4. Thurber has added a moral to the story. What function does the moral of a fable usually have? What's the function of the moral here?
  *5. The poem "Viewing Time" is a parody of "Leisure". Would you describe "The Little Girl and the Wolf" as a parody too? Give reasons.

The peacelike mongoose

In cobra country a mongoose was born one day who didn't want to fight cobras or anything else. The word spread from mongoose to mongoose that there was a mongoose who didn't want to fight cobras. If he didn't want to fight anything else, it was his own business, but it was the duty of every mongoose to kill cobras or be killed by cobras.

"Why?" asked the peacelike mongoose, and the word went around that the strange new mongoose was not only pro-cobra and anti-mongoose but intellectually curious and against the ideals and traditions of mongoosism.

"He is crazy," cried the young mongoose's father.

"He is sick," said his mother.

"He is a coward," shouted his brothers.

"He is a mongoosexual," whispered his sisters.

Strangers who had never laid eyes on the peacelike mongoose remembered that they had seen him crawling on his stomach, or trying on cobra hoods, or plotting the violent overthrow of Mongoosia.

"I am trying to use reason and intelligence," said the strange new mongoose.

"Reason is six-sevenths of treason," said one of his neighbors.

"Intelligence is what the enemy uses," said another.

Finally, the rumor spread that the mongoose had venom in his sting, like a cobra, and he was tried, convicted by a show of paws, and condemned to banishment.

Moral: Ashes to ashes, and clay to clay, if the enemy doesn't get you your own folks may.

James Thurber

- 1. What would you say this fable is about?
  2. What does the peacelike mongoose a) say, b) do?
  3. What is the peacelike mongoose accused of? What evidence are the accusations based on?
  4. Why do you suppose the other mongooses have such strong feelings about the peacelike mongoose that they finally banish him? Is it only because he doesn't want to fight cobras?
  *5. A story or poem written with the aim of criticizing something by making it appear ridiculous is known as a satire. Do you think "The peacelike mongoose" could be called a satire? Give reasons for your opinion.
  6. Even though the author doesn't directly give his opinion about what happens in the story, it's still possible to recognize his attitude. What would you say his attitude was?

Talking about short stories

The beginning, middle and end of a short story have different functions.

The beginning has the function of an *exposition*, i.e. the main theme and characters are introduced.

As the action moves on, *suspense* is created: the reader wants to know what's going to happen next. This is often the result of a *conflict* between the characters.

In the middle section the conflict is built up to a crisis or *climax*, which then demands a solution in the end section.

Sometimes there's a *surprise ending*, sometimes the story is *open-ended*.

A technique often used in short stories is the *flashback*, which tells the reader about events that took place before the story began.

The number of *settings*, events and *characters* in a short story is always limited.

Characterization may be either explicit or implicit.
Explicit characterization is the result of what the author says about a character directly, e.g. Jane was a kind and helpful person. *Implicit* characterization is the result of what a character himself does or says, e.g. Jane: "But of course I can help you. Any time at all." or what others say about him, e.g. John: "Jane is always so kind and helpful."

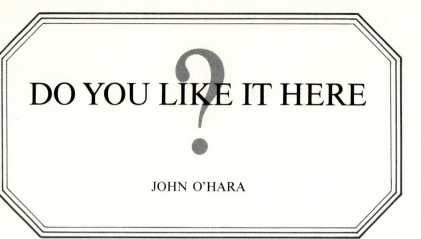

DO YOU LIKE IT HERE

JOHN O'HARA

The door was open. The door had to be kept open during study period, so there was no knock, and Roberts was startled when a voice he knew and hated said, "Hey, Roberts. Wanted in Van Ness's office." The voice was Hughes's.

"What for?" said Roberts.

"Why don't you go and find out what for, Dopey?" said Hughes.

"Phooey on you," said Roberts.

"Phooey on *you*," said Hughes, and left.

Roberts got up from the desk. He took off his eyeshade and put on a tie and coat. He left the light burning.

Van Ness's office, which was *en suite* with his bedroom, was on the ground floor of the dormitory, and on the way down Roberts wondered what he had done. It got so after a while, after going to so many schools, that you recognized the difference between being "wanted in Somebody's office" and "Somebody wants to see you." If a master wanted to see you on some minor matter, it didn't always mean that you had to go to his office; but if it was serious, they always said, "You're wanted in Somebody's office." That meant Somebody would be in his office, waiting for you, waiting specially for you. Roberts didn't know why this difference existed, but it did, all right. Well, all he could think of was that he had been smoking in the shower room, but Van Ness never paid much attention to that. Everybody smoked in the shower room, and Van Ness never did anything about it unless he just happened to catch you.

For minor offences Van Ness would speak to you when he made his rounds of the rooms during study period. He would walk slowly down the corridor, looking in at each room to see that the proper occupant, and no one else, was there; and when he had something to bawl you out about, something unimportant, he would consult a list he carried, and he would stop in and bawl you out about it and tell you what punishment went with it. That was another detail that made the summons to the office a little scary.

Roberts knocked on Van Ness's half-open door and a voice said, "Come in."

Van Ness was sitting at his typewriter, which was on a small desk beside the large desk. He was in a swivel chair and when he saw Roberts he swung around, putting himself behind the large desk, like a damn judge.

He had his pipe in his mouth and he seemed to look over the steel rims of his spectacles. The light caught his Phi Beta Kappa key, which momentarily gleamed as though it had diamonds in it.

"Hughes said you wanted me to report here," said Roberts.

"I did," said Van Ness. He took his pipe out of his mouth and began slowly to knock the bowl empty as he repeated, "I did." He finished emptying his pipe before he again spoke. He took a long time about it, and Roberts, from his years of experience, recognized that as torture tactics. They always made you wait to scare you. It was sort of like the third degree. The horrible damn thing was that it always did scare you a little, even when you were used to it.

Van Ness leaned back in his chair and stared through his glasses at Roberts. He cleared his throat. "You can sit down," he said.

"Yes, sir," said Roberts. He sat down and again Van Ness made him wait.

"Roberts, you've been here now how long – five weeks?"

"A little over. About six."

"About six weeks," said Van Ness. "Since the seventh of January. Six weeks. Strange. Strange. Six weeks, and I really don't know a thing about you. Not much, at any rate. Roberts, tell me a little about yourself."

"How do you mean, Mister?"

"How do I mean? Well – about your life, before you decided to honor us with your presence. Where you came from, what you did, why you went to so many schools, so on."

"Well, I don't know."

"Oh, now. Now, Roberts. Don't let your natural modesty overcome the autobiographical urge. Shut the door."

Roberts got up and closed the door.

"Good," said Van Ness. "Now, proceed with this – uh – dossier. Give me the – huh – huh – *lowdown* on Roberts, Humphrey, Second Form, McAllister Memorial Hall, et cetera."

Roberts, Humphrey, sat down and felt the knot of his tie. "Well, I don't know. I was born at West Point, New York. My father was a first lieutenant

4 A/T

then and he's a major now. My father and mother and I lived in a lot of places because he was in the Army and they transferred him. Is that the kind of stuff you want, Mister?"

"Proceed, proceed. I'll tell you when I want you to – uh – halt." Van Ness seemed to think that was funny, that "halt."

"Well, I didn't go to a regular school till I was ten. My mother got a divorce from my father and I went to school in San Francisco. I only stayed there a year because my mother got married again and we moved to Chicago, Illinois."

"Chicago, Illinois! Well, a little geography thrown in, eh, Roberts? Gratuitously. Thank you. Proceed."

"Well, so then we stayed there about two years and then we moved back East, and my stepfather is a certified public accountant and we moved around a lot."

"Peripatetic, eh, Roberts?"

"I guess so. I don't exactly know what that means." Roberts paused.

"Go on, go on."

"Well, so I just went to a lot of schools, some day and some boarding. All that's written down on my application blank here. I had to put it all down on account of my credits."

"Correct. A very imposing list it is, too, Roberts, a very imposing list. Ah, to travel as you have. Switzerland. How I've regretted not having gone to school in Switzerland. Did you like it there?"

"I was only there about three months. I liked it all right, I guess."

"And do you like it here, Roberts?"

"Sure."

"You do? You're sure of that? You wouldn't want to change anything?"

"Oh, I wouldn't say that, not about any school."

"Indeed," said Van Ness. "With your vast experience, naturally you would be quite an authority on matters educational. I suppose you have many theories as to the strength and weaknesses inherent in the modern educational systems."

"I don't know. I just – I don't know. Some schools are better than others. At least I like some better than others."

"Of course. Of course." Van Ness seemed to be thinking about something. He leaned back in his swivel chair and gazed at the ceiling. He put his hands in his pants pockets and then suddenly he leaned forward. The chair came down and Van Ness's belly was hard against the desk and his arm was stretched out on the desk, full length, fist closed.

"Roberts! Did you ever see this before[+]? Answer me!" Van Ness's voice was hard. He opened his fist, and in it was a wristwatch.

[+] (AE) for (BE) Have you ever seen this before?

Roberts looked down at the watch. "No, I don't think so," he said. He was glad to be able to say it truthfully.

Van Ness continued to hold out his hand, with the wristwatch lying in the palm. He held out his hand a long time, fifteen seconds at least, without saying anything. Then he turned his hand over and allowed the watch to slip onto the desk. He resumed his normal position in the chair. He picked up his pipe, slowly filled it, and lit it. He shook the match back and forth long after the flame had gone. He swung around a little in his chair and looked at the wall, away from Roberts. "As a boy I spent six years at this school. My brothers, my two brothers, went to this school. My *father* went to this school. I have a deep and abiding and lasting affection for this school. I have been a member of the faculty of this school for more than a decade. I like to think that I am part of this school, that in some small measure I have assisted in its progress. I like to think of it as more than a mere steppingstone to higher education. At this very moment there are in this school the sons of men who were my classmates. I have not been without my opportunities to take a post at this and that college or university, but I choose to remain here. Why? Why? Because I love this place. I love this place, Roberts. I cherish its traditions. I cherish its good name." He paused, and turned to Roberts. "Roberts, there is no room here for a thief!"

Roberts did not speak.

"There is no room here for a thief, I said!"

"Yes, sir."

Van Ness picked up the watch without looking at it. He held it a few inches above the desk. "This miserable watch was stolen last Friday afternoon, more than likely during the basketball game. As soon as the theft was reported to me I immediately instituted a search for it. My search was unsuccessful. Sometime Monday afternoon the watch was put here, here in my rooms. When I returned here after classes Monday afternoon, this watch was lying on my desk. Why? Because the contemptible rat who stole it knew that I had instituted the search, and like the rat he is, he turned yellow and returned the watch to me. Whoever it is, he kept an entire dormitory under a loathsome suspicion. I say to you, I do not know who stole this watch, or who returned it to my rooms. But by God, Roberts, I'm going to find out, if it's the last thing I do. If it's the last thing I do. That's all, Roberts. You may go." Van Ness sat back, almost breathless.

Roberts stood up. "I give you my word of honor, I –"

"I said you may go!" said Van Ness.

Roberts was not sure whether to leave the door open or to close it, but he did not ask. He left it open.

He went up the stairs to his room. He went in and took off his coat and tie, and sat on the bed. Over and over again, first violently, then weakly, he said it, "The bastard, the dirty bastard."

4 A/T

- 1. Where, in your opinion, do the three sections of O'Hara's story begin and end? In answering this, it'll help you if you consider the settings.
  2. Can you show how suspense is already being built up in the exposition? (Notice the way Hughes expresses himself.)
  3. How does Van Ness's behaviour in the middle section help to increase the suspense? What role does irony play in his behaviour?
  4. What can you say about the characters of Roberts and Van Ness? Consider a) the two "flashbacks", b) the language used by each of them.
  5. Describe the conflict between the two main characters.
  6. At what point does the climax come? Describe how it's reached.
  7. Is the conflict finally solved? Or would you describe the story as open-ended?
  *8. Comment on the title.

William F. Nolan

AND MILES TO GO BEFORE I SLEEP

Alone within the humming ship, deep in its honeycombed chambers, Robert Murdock waited for death. While the rocket moved inexorably toward Earth – an immense silver needle threading the dark fabric of space – he waited calmly through the final hours, knowing that hope no longer existed.

After twenty years in space, Murdock was going home.

Home. Earth. Thayerville, a small town in Kansas. Clean air, a shaded street and a white two-storey house near the end of the block. Home after two decades among the stars.

The rocket knifed through the black of space, its atomics, like a great heartbeat, pulsing far below Robert Murdock as he sat quietly before a round port, seeing and not seeing the endless darkness surrounding him.

Murdock was remembering.

He remembered the worried face of his mother, her whispered prayers for his safety, the way she held him close for a long, long moment before he mounted the ship's ramp those twenty years ago. He remembered his father: a tall, weathered man, and that last crushing handshake before he said goodbye.

It was almost impossible to realize that they were now old and white-haired, that his father was forced to use a cane, that his mother was bowed and wasted by the years.

And what of himself?

He was now forty-one – and space had weathered him as the plains of Kansas had weathered his father. He, too, had fought storms in his job beyond Earth, terrible, alien storms; worse than any he had ever encountered on his own planet. And he, too, had labored on plains under burning suns far stronger than Sol. His face was square and hard-featured, his eyes dark and buried beneath thrusting ledges of bone.

Robert Murdock removed the stero-shots of his parents from his uniform pocket and studied their faces. Warm, smiling, *waiting* faces: waiting for their son to come home to them. Carefully, he unfolded his mother's last letter. She had always been stubborn about sending tapes, complaining that her voice was unsteady, that she found it so difficult to speak her thoughts into the metallic mouth of a cold, impersonal machine. She insisted on using an

93

4 A/T

old-fashioned pen, forming the words slowly in an almost archaic script. He had received this last letter just before his take-off for Earth, and it read:

Dearest,
We are so excited! Your father and I listened to your voice again and again, telling us that you are coming home to us at last, and we both thanked our good Lord that you were safe. Oh, we are so eager to see you, son. As you know, we have not been too well of late. Your father's heart doesn't allow him to get out much any more. Even the news that you are coming back to us has over-excited him. Then, of course, my own health seems none too good as I suffered another fainting spell last week. But there is no real cause for alarm – and you are not to worry! – since Dr. Thorn says I am still quite strong, and that these spells will pass. I am, however, resting as much as possible, so that I will be fine when you arrive. Please, Bob, come back to us safely. We pray God you will come home safe and well. The thought of you fills our hearts each day. Our lives are suddenly rich again. Hurry, Bob. Hurry!

All our love,
Mother

Robert Murdock put the letter aside and clenched his fists. Only brief hours remained to him – and Earth was *days* away. The town of Thayerville was an impossible distance across space; he knew he could never reach it alive.

Once again, as they had so many times in the recent past, the closing lines of the ancient poem by Robert Frost came whispering through his mind:

But I have promises to keep,
And miles to go before I sleep ...

He'd promised that he would come home, and he would keep that promise. Despite death itself, he would return to Earth.

"*Out of the question!*" the doctors had told him. "*You'll never reach Earth. You'll die out there. You'll die in space.*"

Then they had shown him. They charted his death almost to the final second; they told him when his heart would stop beating, when his breathing would cease. This disease – contracted on an alien world – was incurable. Death, for Robert Murdock, was a certainty.

But he told them he was going home nonetheless, that he was leaving for Earth. And they listened to his plan.

Now, with less than thirty minutes of life remaining, Murdock was walking down one of the ship's long corridors, his bootheels ringing on the metal walkway.

He was ready, at last, to keep his promise.

Pausing before a wall storage-locker, he twisted a small dial. The door slid back. Murdock looked up at the tall man standing motionless in the interior darkness. He reached forward, made a quick adjustment. The tall man spoke. "Is it time?"

"Yes," replied Robert Murdock, "It is time."

The tall man stepped smoothly down into the corridor; the light flashed in the deep-set eyes, almost hidden under thrusting ledges of bone. The man's face was hard and square-featured. "You see," he smiled, "I *am* perfect."

"And so you are," said Murdock. But then, he reflected, everything *depends* on perfection. There must be no flaw, however small. None.

"My name is Robert Murdock," said the tall figure in the neat spaceman's uniform. "I am forty-one years of age, sound of mind and body. I have been in space for two decades – and now I am going home."

Murdock smiled, a tight smile of triumph which flickered briefly across his tired face.

"How much longer?" the tall figure asked.

"Ten minutes. Perhaps a few seconds beyond that," said Murdock slowly. "They told me it would be painless."

"Then ..." The tall man paused, drew in a long breath. "I'm sorry."

Murdock smiled again. He knew that a machine, however perfect, could not experience the emotion of sorrow – but it eased him to hear the words.

He'll be fine, thought Murdock. He'll serve in my place and my parents will never suspect that I have not come home to them. A month, as arranged, and the machine would turn itself in to company officials on Earth. Yes, Murdock thought, he will be fine.

"Remember," said Murdock, "when you leave them, they *must* believe you are going back into space."

"Naturally," said the machine. And Murdock listened to his own voice explain: "When the month I am to stay with them has passed, they'll see me board a rocket. They'll see it fire away from Earth, outbound, and they'll know that I cannot return for two more decades. They will accept the fact that their son must return to space – that a healthy spaceman cannot leave the Service until he has reached sixty. Let me assure you, all will go exactly as you have planned."

It *will* work, Murdock told himself; every detail has been taken into consideration. The android possesses every memory that I possess; his voice is *my* voice, his small habits my own. And when he leaves them, when it appears that he has gone back to the stars, the pre-recorded tapes of mine will continue to reach them from space, exactly as they have in the past. Until their deaths. They will never know I'm gone, thought Robert Murdock.

"Are you ready now?" the tall figure asked softly.

"Yes," said Murdock, nodding. "I'm ready."

And they began to walk slowly down the long corridor.

4 A/T

Murdock remembered how proud his parents had been when he was accepted for Special Service. He had been the only boy in the entire town of Thayerville to be chosen. It had been a great day! The local band playing, the mayor – old Mr Harkness with those little glasses tilted across his nose – making a speech, telling everyone how proud Thayerville was of its chosen son ... and his mother crying because she was so happy.

But then, it was only right that he should have gone into space. The other boys, the ones who failed to make the grade, had not *lived* the dream as he had lived it. From the moment he had watched the first moon rocket land, he had known, beyond any possible doubt, that he would become a spaceman. He had stood there, in that cold December of 1980, a boy of twelve, watching the rocket fire down from space, watching it thaw and blacken the frozen earth. And he had known, in his heart, that he would one day follow it back to the stars. From that moment on, he had dreamed only of moving up and away from Earth, away to vast and alien horizons, to wondrous worlds beyond imagining.

And many of the others had been unwilling to give up *everything* for space. Even now, after two decades, he could still hear Julie's words: *"Oh, I'm sure you love me, Bob, but not enough. Not nearly enough to give up your dream."* And she had left him, gone out of his life because she knew there was no room in it for her. There was only space – deep space and the rockets and the burning stars. Nothing else.

He remembered his last night on Earth, twenty years ago, when he had felt the pressing immensity of the vast universe surrounding him as he lay in his bed. He remembered the sleepless hours before dawn – when he could feel the tension building within the small white house, within himself lying there in the heated stillness of the room. He remembered the rain, near morning, drumming the roof and the thunder roaring across the Kansas sky. And then, somehow, the thunder's roar blended into the atomic roar of a rocket, carrying him away from Earth, away to the far stars ... away ...

Away.

The tall figure in the neat spaceman's uniform closed the outer airlock and watched the body drift into blackness. The ship and the android were one; a pair of complex and perfect machines doing their job.

For Robert Murdock, the journey was over, the long miles had come to an end. Now he would sleep forever in space.

When the rocket landed, on a bright morning in July, in Thayerville, Kansas, the crowds were there, waving and shouting out Robert Murdock's name. The city officials were all present to the last man, each with a carefully rehearsed speech in his mind; the town band sent brassy music into the blue

4

sky and children waved flags. Then a hush fell over the assembled throng. The atomic engines had stilled and the airlock was sliding back.

Robert Murdock appeared, tall and heroic in a splendid dress uniform which threw back the light of the sun in a thousand glittering patterns. He smiled and waved as the crowd burst into fresh shouting and applause.

And, at the far end of the ramp, two figures waited: an old man, bowed and trembling over a cane, and a seamed and wrinkled woman, her hair blowing white, her eyes shining.

When the tall man finally reached them, pushing his way through pressing lines of well-wishers, they embraced him feverishly. They clung tight to his arms as he walked between them; they looked up at him with tears in their eyes.

Robert Murdock, their beloved son, had come home to them at last.

4 A/T

"Well," said a man at the fringe of the crowd, "there they go."

His companion sighed and shook his head. "I *still* don't think it's right, somehow. It just doesn't seem right to me."

"It's what they wanted, isn't it?" asked the other. "It's what they put in their wills. They vowed their son would never come home to death. In another month he'll be gone anyway. Back for twenty more years. Why spoil what little time he has, why ruin it all for him?" The man paused, indicating the two figures in the near distance. "They're *perfect*, aren't they? He'll never know."

"I guess you're right," agreed the second man. "He'll never know."

And he watched the old man and the old woman and the tall son until they were out of sight.

- 1. Try and divide the story into its three sections: exposition, middle section and end. In doing this, it'll help if you first make a note of all the flashbacks. How many are there?
- 2. At the end of the exposition what do we know about a) Robert Murdock, b) his parents? What question does the reader ask himself at this point?
- 3. In the long middle section the author creates suspense by slowly adding more and more details of Murdock's plan. What is his plan? What does the reader ask himself now?
- 4. Describe Murdock's character and compare him to his parents. How do their characters contribute to the way the story ends? What techniques does the author use to characterize them?
- 5. Towards the end the suspense is increased by the word "it" being repeated four times (in lines 2 to 4 on this page). At what exact point do we learn the truth? Do you find the ending convincing? Give reasons to support your opinion.
- 6. The story takes place in the future and describes things that may or may not ever really happen. It's an example of science fiction. What elements in the story belong to science fiction in your opinion? How do these elements contribute to the interpretation of the story?
- 7. What about the human beings? Do they think, feel or behave in any way differently from people today?
- *8. Some lines from Robert Frost's poem "Stopping by woods on a snowy evening" are quoted in the title and again in the text. What parallels and differences can you see between the poem and the story?

4 Ex

Here are three further pieces of writing: 1. a poem, 2. a very short short story, and 3. a fable. Write one or two paragraphs about 1. and 2., referring to the notes on pages 76 and 87.

1   **Little Johnny's confession**

This morning
    being rather young and foolish
    I borrowed a machinegun my father
    had left hidden since the war, went out,
    and eliminated a number of small enemies.
    Since then I have not returned home.

This morning   This morning
    swarms of police with trackerdogs   sitting alone in a strange playground,
    wander about the city   muttering Youve blundered Youve blundered
    with my description printed   over and over to myself
    on their minds, asking: I work out my next move
    'Have you seen him,   but cannot move;
    He is seven years old,   the trackerdogs will sniff me out,
    likes Pluto, Mighty Mouse   they have my lollypops.
    and Biffo The Bear,
    have you seen him, anywhere?'   *Brian Patten*

2   *I can tell wops a mile off*

    At two o'clock in the morning two Hungarians got into a cigar store at Fifteenth Street and Grand Avenue. Drevitts and Boyle drove up from the Fifteenth Street police station in a Ford. The Hungarians were backing
5   their wagon out of an alley. Boyle shot one off the seat of the wagon and one out of the wagon box. Drevitts got frightened when he found they were both dead.
    "Hell, Jimmy," he said, "you oughtn't to have done it. There's liable to be a hell of a lot of trouble."
10   "They're crooks, ain't they?" said Boyle. "They're wops, ain't they? Who the hell is going to make any trouble?"
    "That's all right maybe this time," said Drevitts, "but how did you know they were wops when you bumped them off?"
    "Wops," said Boyle, "I can tell wops a mile off."
15   *Ernest Hemingway*

4 Ex

3 Write one or two paragraphs about this fable, comparing it with the one on page 86.

The rabbits who caused all the trouble

Within the memory of the youngest child there was a family of rabbits who lived near a pack of wolves. The wolves announced that they did not like the way the rabbits were living. (The wolves were crazy about the way they themselves were living, because it was the only way to live.) One night several wolves were killed in an earthquake and this was blamed on the rabbits, for it is well known that rabbits pound on the ground with their hind legs and cause earthquakes. On another night one of the wolves was killed by a bolt of lightning and this was also blamed on the rabbits, for it is well known that lettuce-eaters cause lightning. The wolves threatened to civilize the rabbits if they didn't behave, and the rabbits decided to run away to a desert island. But the other animals, who lived at a great distance, shamed them, saying, 'You must stay where you are and be brave. This is no world for escapists. If the wolves attack you, we will come to your aid, in all probability.' So the rabbits continued to live near the wolves and one day there was a terrible flood which drowned a great many wolves. This was blamed on the rabbits, for it is well known that carrot-nibblers with long ears cause floods. The wolves descended on the rabbits, for their own good, and imprisoned them in a dark cave, for their own protection.

When nothing was heard about the rabbits for some weeks, the other animals demanded to know what had happened to them. The wolves replied that the rabbits had been eaten and since they had been eaten the affair was a purely internal matter. But the other animals warned that they might possibly unite against the wolves unless some reason was given for the destruction of the rabbits. So the wolves gave them one. 'They were trying to escape,' said the wolves, 'and, as you know, this is no world for escapists.'

Moral: Run, don't walk, to the nearest desert island.

James Thurber

4 Simple present – present progressive

Finish these conversations by making up a response with the help of the pictures. Use such adverbials as: *this week/month/year, for a change, instead.*

1. *Mr Johnson:* I thought you went to work by car, Mr Feather?
   Mr Feather: Yes, I usually do. But I had an accident. So I'm going by bus this week.
2. *Pamela:* I thought you always had lunch in the Indian restaurant, Janet?
   Janet: Well, I normally do. But it's closed from .... So I'm ....
3. *Bruce:* I thought you and Sarah played tennis on Sunday mornings, Ben?
   Ben: We .... But .... So we're ....
4. *Neighbour:* I thought you and Herb always went to Spain for your holidays, Liz?
5. *Husband:* I thought you went to choir practice on Tuesdays, love?
6. *Neighbour:* I thought you went to church on Sunday mornings, Tom?

4

5 Simple present – present progressive

> *Here are some ways of talking about the present.*
>
> *simple present*
> Sarah **plays** tennis every Saturday. (a habit)
> I **don't know** if I **like** this film. (mental/emotional states)
>
> *present progressive*
> I**'m reading** the paper at the moment. (something in progress)
> My father **is staying** late at work this week. (something temporary)

Fill in the correct forms in this conversation.

Janet: Hallo, Mike.	
Mike: Hallo, Janet. I haven't seen you for ages. How's life? You've changed your job, haven't you? Where *are.* you *working* these days?	work
Janet: For BTX, the company that … pocket calculators. I'm a secretary. Not a bad job really, I … .	make suppose
Mike: … you … the work?	like
Janet: Yes, I … quite a lot of people, and the company … good wages. I … this week especially because the boss is away. But the thing is, I … a job with more responsibility if I can get one. Secretaries … the dirty work for the men, I … .	meet pay, enjoy want just do reckon
Mike: Have you applied for another job?	
Janet: No, but I … at the ads in the paper at the moment. What about you? Didn't someone tell me you … for a job?	look still look
Mike: I've found some temporary work now. I … a van for a greengrocer. It's good because I … driving, but I … it for a month during the holiday period. Look, Janet, … you … anything just at the moment? Have you got time for a cup of tea?	drive like only do do
Janet: I've got to be back at work by two, but I … I'll have time. I'd love one anyway.	think
Mike: Come on then.	

6 Present perfect: simple and progressive forms

Put the verbs in brackets into the simple or progressive forms of the present perfect.

Steve: Hallo, Chris. I (wait) for you for half an hour. What (do) you?
Chris: Sorry. I (help) Pete Perrott to learn his German irregular verbs since four o'clock and I (come) straight here. It's his last exam tomorrow.
Steve: (Bring) you that holiday brochure about Cornwall?
Chris: No. I (send) away for it, but it (not come) yet. – Look, do you want another hamburger with me, or shall we go now?
Steve: Go already? But I thought Elaine was coming too. She (finish) her O-levels now, hasn't she?
Chris: Yes, but she (show) foreign tourists round the town all the week and she's exhausted in the evenings. Take today – she (take) six groups round the sights since lunch time.
Steve: I wish I had a girl like Elaine. You (go) out with her for ages now, haven't you?
Chris: Well, I (know) her for ages but, funnily enough, I (go) out with her for less than a year. Are you sure you won't have a hamburger?
Steve: No, really. I already (eat) five or six this evening. It's a kind of nervous reaction to the exams. Thank goodness they're all over soon.
Chris: You can say that again. How long (do) we exams now? Four weeks?
Steve: Must be. Only Latin to come now though. Do you reckon you (pass) all yours, Chris?
Chris: Hope so, but I won't relax till I (hear) all the results.

7 Simple past – past progressive

Put the verbs in brackets into the simple past or past progressive.

One Friday evening Arthur Maxwell M.P. (drive) back along the motorway to his constituency when he (notice) he (not have) his watch. "Damn it!" he (think), "I wonder how I (forget) it. What (do) I when I (take) it off? Oh, of course, I (expect) visitors at four, so I (put) the watch in front of me on the desk while I (deal) with all my correspondence." To find out the time he (turn) on his car radio. The news (read, **passive**), so he (know) it (be) a few minutes past ten.
Arthur Maxwell always (enjoy) his weekends, but he (look) forward to this one more than usual as it had been a particularly hard week at Westminster. Thirty minutes later he (arrive) home. His wife (have) a drink and (read) the paper, his daughter (listen) to records in her room. When they (hear) him come in, though, they (stop) what they (do) and (join) him for a chat before going to bed.

4 Ex

8 Present/present perfect/past – simple and progressive forms

Put in the right form of the verbs.

Esperanto

People *haven't yet given up* hope that the whole world will one day speak a common language. For a long time now people ... new languages with this aim. At least 600 such languages ... in the search for a second or auxiliary language which all human beings would be able to speak. The most famous one, Esperanto, was the idea of a man called Ludwig Zamenhof, who ... in Warsaw as a doctor when he ... a book explaining his new language in 1887. Zamenhof ... under the name Dr Esperanto – 'Esperanto' ... 'one who hopes'. Zamenhof ... that a common second language would help people to understand each other and reduce the risk of wars.	not yet give up make up develop (passive) work publish write mean, hope
In order to encourage people to learn the language, he ... it as simple as possible. For example, all nouns in the singular ... in 'o' and in the plural in 'oj', verbs in the present tense in 'as' and in the past in 'is'. Everything is regular.	make end
Esperanto and other new languages ... a lot of attention in the 20-30 years after 1887, but this ... a time when the great powers ... for the conflict of 1914-1918.	attract be prepare
Esperanto ... as an official world language, and since it ... as an auxiliary language there ... two world wars. However, by 1950 it ... 1½ million speakers and ... in 600 schools. Today Esperanto ... by about 8 million people, and more than one hundred newspapers and magazines in the language ... regularly throughout the world. Thousands of books ... in Esperanto, including those translated from other languages.	never accept (pass.) suggest (pass.), be have, teach (pass.) speak (pass.) publish (pass.) write (pass.)
But these days the need for a new auxiliary language like Esperanto ... less obvious. Throughout this century English ... more and more important, and it ... a second language for many millions of people. Millions of pupils ... English at this moment and the world-wide use of English ... . No-one would deny the usefulness of a world language, but not many people ... that Esperanto is now likely to play such a role.	seem grow, become learn still grow think

9 Will-future – present progressive

> *will-future*
> **I'll be** eighteen next week. (something that will happen anyway)
> I've got an idea – **I'll have** a party on Sunday. (a sudden decision)
> I'm sure it**'ll be** a good party. (an opinion)
>
> *present progressive*
> They**'re holding** a meeting at four tomorrow. (a definite arrangement)

Fill in the correct forms in this conversation.

There's a festival of literature this week in the town where Graham and Carol live. They're looking at today's programme for the festival.

Carol:	I think I'*ll visit* the book exhibition that'*s opening* at the school this afternoon.	visit open
Graham:	Not me. I … with Anne to the sale of old library books at the town hall. There … lots of cheap books there.	go be
Carol:	I … you there later. – Oh, what about this? Hilary Sleek and Vanessa Partington-Holmes … some of their poems this lunch time.	probably see read
Graham:	I've never heard of them. I expect I … lunch at home.	have
Carol:	Then Mike Thrubb … a talk this afternoon. I bet he … about his new novel.	give talk
Graham:	… you … to that?	go
Carol:	Yes, I'm keen on Mike Thrubb.	
Graham:	I see that this evening experts from the TV programme 'World of Books' … some new books. I … Anne to that, too, I think.	discuss take
Carol:	You … get there early. It … full. I reckon I … Martin Speedwell. He … to the audience how to write a novel.	have to, be listen to, explain
Graham:	Why, … you … to write a novel when you leave school?	plan
Carol:	When I leave school? I've started the first page already.	

105

4 Ex

Communication practice: *Avoiding bluntness*

1. Compare the way these two teachers tell a pupil her answer is wrong:

   Teacher A: Really, Susan. What a stupid answer! If you can't think of anything more intelligent to say, you'd better keep quiet.

   Teacher B: Well, Susan, I'm not sure that your answer is completely right. Haven't you forgotten something? Can anyone help her?

   Teacher A's words are, of course, rude. Nobody should speak like that. Teacher B, however, is not simply polite, he avoids saying directly what he means. He says it indirectly in order to avoid being blunt.

2. English people really seem to enjoy expressing themselves in an indirect way. At least, they often do so where a foreigner wouldn't expect it at all, for example when making a complaint about something. Here are some indirect ways of saying things.

Instead of:	You can say:
Don't do that.	I wouldn't do that if I were you.
Wait here.	Would you mind waiting here?
Can I ...?	I'm terribly sorry to bother you, but could I possibly ...?
Do you want to ...?	I was wondering whether you might like to ....
I disagree.	I'm not sure that I altogether agree.
That's a silly point.	That's a good point. On the other hand ....
awful/expensive/ugly	not exactly fantastic/cheap/beautiful

3. Can you make the following remarks more typically English?

   Woman (to waiter): Where's my salad? Bring it at once, please.
   Man (in discussion): What rubbish! I disagree completely.
   Boy (to new girl): Do you want to come with me to the cinema tonight?
   Man (to driver parked in his entrance): Move your car, please.
   Girl (to friend): Tony Hill is a rotten dancer, I must say.

4. Now make up some short dialogues in which the first speaker avoids being blunt. Some possible responses, which you already know, are:
   Not at all./But of course./I'd be delighted./Do you really think so?
   1. Martha thinks she should have got a better mark in her maths test. She complains to her teacher. – 2. The coach tells Liz the bad news: she's not in the team this week. – 3. After his father's car has had a break-down in a country area, Tom knocks on the door of the nearest house to ask if he can use the phone. – 4. Mr Old complains to the manager about his cold hotel room. – 5. Mr Bell disagrees with his boss about immigrants.

4 S

Revision: Simple and progressive forms in different tenses

1 Simple present and present progressive

a The simple present is used

1. to talk about habits:

Sally **spends** her holidays at the seaside. (i.e. usually/generally/often)
Does Bob always **sing** in the choir on Tuesdays? – I **don't read** comics.

2. to talk about what is permanent or characteristic, i.e. not temporary or likely to change:

France **lies** to the west of Germany. – The church **stands** on a hill.
Mr Black **sells** sausages. His wife **doesn't work**. – **Do** you **study** French?
Cows **eat** grass. – Pigs **don't fly**. – Supersonic planes **make** a lot of noise.
Tony **speaks** excellent French. – **Does** Anne **play** the piano very well?

3. to talk about a text, letter, play, film, etc.:

What **happens** in the story? – The first paragraph **describes** a spring day.
What **does** Jane **write** in her letter? – The film **deals** with Europe.

4. for instructions:

How do I get to the station? You **go** straight on, then **turn** left at the bank. After that you **take** the second road on the right.

5. in adverbial clauses of time referring to the future:

Will you meet Susan when she **arrives**? – We can't leave till Pete **comes**.
I want to go for a walk as soon as it **stops** raining.

6. to refer to a timetable or a definite programme of future events:

We **arrive** on Saturday, **stay** two nights, then **leave** on Monday morning.
Exams **begin** on Friday, 21st. – Bob Dylan **appears** in Berlin on the 29th.

7. with a number of different verbs not normally used in the progressive, e.g. verbs of "saying": *say, ask, deny, advise, warn, wonder, admit*, etc.;
with verbs expressing a state: *belong, consist, depend, matter, own, seem*;
in particular an emotional state: *hate, hope, (dis)like, love, mind, prefer*;
or a mental state: *think, imagine, suppose, know, understand, remember*, etc.

Note: the verbs of perception (*see, hear, smell, taste*) are also not usually used in the progressive.

b The present progressive is used

1. for something which is in progress, i.e. which is not yet over:

John **is washing** his hands at the moment. – What **are** you **doing** there?
Oh look, it**'s snowing**. – **Are** you **enjoying** yourself? – It**'s getting** dark.

2. for something which is in progress but is interrupted for a time:

(in the street) Hi, Pete! Sorry I can't stop – I**'m painting** the bedroom.
(on the phone) What are you doing? – We**'re playing** darts.
(on a bus) Hi, Al! Finished your article yet? – No, I**'m** still **writing** it.

3. for something which – even if repeated – is only temporary, i.e. not permanent:

While my car is being repaired, I**'m using** the bus. – Ron lives in London, but during his stay in Germany, he**'s living** with a family in Stuttgart. My watch is normally excellent, but this week it **isn't working** too well. Due to the bad weather all planes **are arriving** late today.

4. for definite future arrangements or plans:

Lynn **is taking** the children to the zoo tomorrow. – No, I**'m not doing** anything special on the 1st. – Where **are** you **going** on holiday this year? Ed **is doing** A-levels next June. – Not another drink, thanks, I**'m driving**.

(5.) There's a special use of the present progressive with *always* meaning *extremely often* (in the speaker's opinion). In such sentences *always* usually carries a strong stress. Compare:

Al always **eats** in posh restaurants. (= every time he eats out)
Al **is** 'always **eating** in posh restaurants. (= extremely often in my opinion)

2 Present perfect and present perfect progressive

a The (simple) present perfect is used

1. to refer to the present result of something that took place in the past at some unmentioned time:

I**'ve bought** a new moped. Look, do you like it? – Jill **has done** her work, so now she can relax, but Sue **hasn't finished** hers. – The Greens **have gone** shopping, so there's nobody at home now.

2. in sentences that refer to a period of time beginning in the past and extending to the present, but without a particular point of time being mentioned. Typical adverbials are *always, ever, never, this week/month/year, already* (in statements), *yet* (in questions and negative sentences):

Have you ever **been** to England? – Liz **has** always **written** untidily. – We**'ve** already **done** three tests this week, but Angela's class **haven't done** any yet. – I**'ve seen** most of O'Neill's films more than once, but I**'ve** never **seen** his first film.

b The present perfect progressive is used

1. to refer to an action that began in the past, is still going on and may continue into the future. Common adverbials are *since* + point of time, *for* + period of time, *all day/the week, How long ... ?*:

I've been learning English for six years now/since 1974. – How long **have** you **been taking** driving lessons? – It**'s been growing** colder all the week.

Compare: I**'ve been writing** letters all day. (an activity that may go on)
  I**'ve written** six letters today. (the result of an activity)

Note: verbs not generally used in the progressive (see § 1a 7.) + be and *have got* are also not used in the present perfect progressive.

(2.) The present perfect progressive is sometimes used to refer to an activity that is already over, but whose unintended effects are still present, e.g.:

My back is aching because I**'ve been working** in the garden all day. (The work may have finished hours earlier.)

Compare: I**'ve cleaned** my shoes. Look how clean they are.
  I**'ve been cleaning** my shoes. Look how dirty my hands are.

3 Simple past and past progressive

a The simple past is used

to refer to something that took place at a particular point of time in the past, or during a period of time that finished in the past. This must be clear either from the adverbials in the sentence (e.g. *... ago, in ..., at ..., last ..., when ..., When ... ?*), or from the context:

These events all **happened** fifty years ago. – My grandfather **died** in 1970. **Did** you **hear** the news at ten? – When I **was** little, I **lived** in Brighton. I like your coat. When **did** you **buy** it? – Oh, lightning! **Did** you **see** it? A man **came** into the room, **looked** round nervously, then **went** out again.

b The past progressive is used

1. to show that something was already in progress at a particular point of time in the past:

When I got home, my parents **were watching** TV. – What **were** you **doing** when I came in and interrupted you? – Kate fell and broke her leg while she **was skating**. – I didn't start working at six, I **was** already **working** then.

Compare: When I got home, my father **made** tea. (He began when I arrived.)
  When I got home, my father **was making** tea. (He'd begun before I arrived.)

(2.) to emphasize that something didn't simply take place, but lasted throughout the period of time mentioned:

I **was tidying** my room all day Sunday. – They **were cooking** and **washing** up from six till eight. – What **were** you **doing** yesterday afternoon?

Translation practice

Unit 1 Veränderung der Wortart

1. **Substantiv im Englischen – Adjektiv oder Verb im Deutschen**

   A stranger *asked me the way.* – *He was a* stranger *to me.*
   Ein Fremder fragte mich nach dem Weg. – Er war mir fremd.

   Wie das zweite Beispiel zeigt, läßt sich ein englisches Substantiv nicht immer stilistisch angemessen auch im Deutschen mit einem Substantiv wiedergeben. Je nach Zusammenhang bietet sich als Ausweg die Übersetzung durch ein Adjektiv oder ein Verb an. Natürlich müssen dann auch andere Teile des Satzes verändert werden. Hierfür ein Beispiel:

   His importance *to his mother is quite obvious.*
   Daß er seiner Mutter viel bedeutet, ist ganz offensichtlich.

   Dies ist auch bei der Übersetzung der folgenden Sätze zu beachten:
   a) *After taking lessons for a few months she was quite a good* pianist.
   b) *Since she had lost the recipe, she made a complete* mess *of the dinner.*
   c) *"I can show you a* variety *of saws," the owner of the shop said.*
   d) *He practised a lot and soon became a very fast* reader.

2. **Verb im Englischen – Adverb im Deutschen**

   Das Prinzip, bei der Übersetzung mitunter eine andere Wortart wählen zu müssen, trifft nicht nur auf Substantive, sondern beispielsweise auch auf eine Reihe englischer Verben zu. Sie sind oft durch ein deutsches Adverb wiederzugeben:

   He happened *to meet her again in London.*
   Zufällig traf er sie in London wieder.

   Don't keep *asking me such stupid questions.*
   Stell mir doch nicht dauernd so dumme Fragen!

   It continued *snowing all day.*
   Es schneite den ganzen Tag weiter.

   Wie lassen sich in den folgenden Sätzen *might/used to* übersetzen?
   a) *I* might *return earlier.*   b) *He* used to *live on the outskirts of Leeds.*

   Auch gewisse Fügungen des Typs *be* + Adjektiv können mit Hilfe von Adverbien übersetzt werden, z. B.

   Old Jim is certain *to know the answer.*
   Der alte Jim weiß die Antwort bestimmt.

   I'm sorry I can't come.
   Ich kann leider nicht kommen.

Bei der Übersetzung der folgenden Sätze kommt es ebenfalls auf die Wahl der passenden Adverbien an:

a) *Oh, I'm* sure *you're right.*   b) *Tom* enjoys *discussing political affairs.*
c) *Jill* prefers *watching TV.*   d) *I* suppose *I must write the letter again.*

Übung

1. *The teacher played the song on a record-player because he wasn't a good singer.*   2. *Her* name *was Black before she married, and now* it's *White.*   3. *Because of the* lateness *of their arrival, the meeting was cancelled.*   4. *Years of experience have shown that quick progress is rarely possible.*   5. *West Germans are the world's biggest beer-*drinkers.   6. *I haven't got enough money, I'*m afraid.   7. *Let's hope the weather doesn't get even worse.*   8. Didn't there use to *be a cinema on this corner?*   9. *The government* aren't likely *to know how to deal with the problem, but they'*re sure *to say they do.*   10. *That* may *be the best plan.*

Unit 2   Infinitive (III)

In einem vorangegangenen Kapitel wurden Infinitive des Typs: *He bought a magazine to read on the trip.* behandelt. Dabei wurden zwei Übersetzungsmöglichkeiten vorgestellt:

a) Relativsatz: ... Zeitschrift, die er auf der Reise lesen wollte/konnte.
b) Substantivfügung: ... Zeitschrift als Reiselektüre.

1. Wenn dem Infinitiv ein Subjekt mit *for* vorausgeht, können diese beiden Varianten ebenfalls benutzt werden:

   He bought a magazine for her to read on the trip.
   a) ... Zeitschrift, die sie ...   b) ... Zeitschrift für sie als ...
   ... ihr eine Zeitschrift als ...

   Daneben lassen sich solche Infinitive oft mit einem „(so) daß/damit"-Satz übersetzen:

   c) ..., (so) daß/damit sie auf der Fahrt etwas zu lesen hätte.

   Bei der Übersetzung folgender Sätze ist an alle Varianten zu denken:
   a) *Here's a list of things for you to buy.*   b) *I've been waiting since breakfast for Mary to phone me.*   c) *Mrs King made a new dress for her daughter to wear at her birthday party.*   d) *Here's a map for you to follow our route.*

2. Bei der Übersetzung dieser Struktur in Verbindung mit Adjektiven sind folgende Wiedergabemöglichkeiten zu beachten:

111

a) nach *too* + Adjektiv

This box is too heavy for you to carry.
Du kannst diese Kiste nicht tragen. Sie ist zu schwer für dich.
(Auflösung in zwei Sätze)
Oder: Diese Kiste ist zu schwer für dich. (Auslassung des Infinitivs)
Oder: Diese Kiste ist zu schwer, als daß du sie tragen könntest.
(„als daß"-Satz, eher schriftsprachlich verwendet)

b) nach Adjektiv + *enough*

The book is easy enough for a little child to understand.
Das Buch ist so leicht, daß es (sogar) ein kleines Kind verstehen kann.
(„daß"-Satz mit vorausgehendem „so")

Übung

1. *The teacher prepared a list of topics for the class to discuss.* 2. *Let's wait for all the others to get back.* 3. *The questions were too complex for most candidates to answer properly.* 4. *Most road signs are clear enough for foreigners to understand quite easily.* 5. *The new model is far too expensive for most people to be able to afford.* 6. *Have you arranged for Mike and Jenny to meet us when we arrive?* 7. *There was nothing for the children to play with while they waited.* 8. *How important is it for Britain to stay in the Common Market in your opinion?* 9. *Their policies were attractive enough for many people to vote for the new party.* 10. *The result was announced in front of the town hall for all to hear.* 11. *Mr and Mrs Freeman were looking for somebody to look after their children.*

Unit 3   Partizipien (II)

In einem vorausgehenden Abschnitt dieses Übersetzungskursus wurde die Wiedergabe nachgestellter englischer Partizipien behandelt, z. B.:

The four girls injured in the accident were taken to hospital.
People living near the scene of the explosion heard a terrible noise.

Im folgenden sollen Übersetzungsmöglichkeiten für andere Partizipialkonstruktionen vorgestellt werden.

1. Bekanntlich kann im Englischen ein Partizip anstelle eines adverbialen Nebensatzes verwendet werden. Steht vor dem Partizip eine Konjunktion, bietet die Übersetzung kaum Schwierigkeiten, z. B.:

Though recognizing the difficulties, they decided to go on.
Obwohl sie die Schwierigkeiten erkannten, beschlossen sie weiterzumachen.

While watching the game, I suddenly remembered my mother's birthday.
Während ich dem Spiel zuschaute, dachte ich plötzlich an den Geburtstag meiner Mutter.

Fehlt dagegen die Konjunktion, so ist aus dem Kontext zu erschließen, ob es sich z.B. um einen temporalen oder kausalen Nebensatz handelt, damit die passende deutsche Konjunktion gewählt werden kann:

Having listened patiently to his opponent's arguments, the Tory candidate began his speech.
Not knowing which way to go, I asked somebody the way.

2. *The disappointed fans left the stadium shouting and burning their flags.*
Die enttäuschten Fans verließen das Stadion, wobei sie schrien und ihre Fahnen verbrannten.

Complete the exercise using -ing forms.
Ergänze die Übung, indem du ing-Formen verwendest.

In diesen Sätzen werden durch die Partizipien die Begleitumstände, unter denen sich die Handlung des Hauptsatzes vollzieht, ausgedrückt. Sie können im Deutschen durch Nebensätze, die mit „wobei" oder „indem" eingeleitet werden, wiedergegeben werden.

Tom sat in the garden dreaming about his holidays.
Tom saß im Garten und träumte von seinen Ferien.

Vielfach ist es aus stilistischen Gründen jedoch angemessener, das Partizip durch „und" + zweites Hauptverb zu ersetzen.

Besonders hinzuweisen ist auf die Übersetzung eines Präsenspartizips, das auf *come* folgt, z.B.:

He came running into the garden.
Er kam in den Garten gerannt.

3. Auch wenn der Partizipialsatz ein eigenes Subjekt hat, bietet sich die Übersetzung durch einen Nebensatz an:

I can't sleep with you laughing all the time.
Ich kann nicht schlafen, wenn du die ganze Zeit lachst.

The girl suddenly ran out of the room, her face hidden in her hands.
Das Mädchen lief plötzlich aus dem Zimmer. Das Gesicht hielt sie in ihren Händen verborgen.

4. Einige Partizipien sind zu formelhaften Ausdrücken geworden. Sie können entweder durch einen deutschen Nebensatz oder vergleichbare Fügungen wiedergegeben werden, z. B. *Generally speaking,* ... (Im allgemeinen ...); *Talking of money,* ... (Da wir gerade von Geld sprechen, ...).

Übung

1. *Strictly speaking, BBC English is a social dialect.* 2. *We can't go on holiday with the car making a noise like that.* 3. *The painter finished the job in one day, working from 6am to 10pm.* 4. *Realizing it was useless to continue, the girls decided to go back.* 5. *Having no more money left, Tim had to borrow some.* 6. *We stood on the corner waiting for the bus.* 7. *How can anybody work with you talking all the time?* 8. *As I looked out of the window, a little bird came flying past.* 9. *They left the concert trying to be as quiet as possible.* 10. *She opened the letter, smiling.* 11. *Circumstances permitting, the books will be delivered in August.*

Unit 4   Die Übersetzung längerer Texte

1. Ehe man beginnt, einen längeren Text zu übersetzen, sollte man ihn mindestens zweimal ganz durchlesen, um den Aufbau und die Hauptgedanken zu erfassen. Beim zweiten Lesen kann man Textstellen, die man nicht verstanden hat, durch Unterstreichen, Fragezeichen usw. kenntlich machen (aber Vorsicht bei geliehenen Büchern!).
2. Fertigt man einen Rohentwurf an, so sollte man entweder einen breiten Rand oder Leerzeilen lassen; auf diese Weise können später Verbesserungen eingefügt werden.
3. Es empfiehlt sich, zunächst nur die Sätze bzw. Teilsätze zu übersetzen, die keine Schwierigkeiten bereiten. Erst danach sollte man an die Wiedergabe der schwierigen Stellen gehen, für die Lücken gelassen wurden.
4. Die Überschrift übersetzt man am besten zuletzt, weil zu ihrem Verständnis meist die genaue Kenntnis des Gesamttextes gehört. Auch für die angemessene Übersetzung anderer Textteile erweist sich oft der Blick über den Einzelsatz hinaus als sinnvoll.
5. Beim Übersetzen versteht man zwar häufig den Sinn eines Einzelwortes, findet aber nicht sofort den angemessenen deutschen Ausdruck. In diesem Fall ist es ratsam, ein Wort zu wählen, das zumindest sinngemäß paßt, es zu kennzeichnen und erst nach Beendigung der Rohübersetzung durch einen geeigneteren Ausdruck zu ersetzen.
6. Hat man mehrere deutsche Wörter für ein englisches Wort zur Verfügung, so führt man sie alle auf und trifft während der stilistischen Überarbeitungsphase die endgültige Auswahl.

Es folgen Beispiele für die Anwendung einiger dieser Arbeitshilfen mit Bezug auf die Übersetzung des nachstehenden Textes.

Zu 4.: Die Übersetzung der Überschrift geht aus dem letzten Abschnitt des Textes hervor. *Social accent* (Zeile 17) wird erst durch die folgenden Sätze wirklich verständlich; dagegen muß bei dem Satz *"Education has helped too."* (Zeile 13) auf den vorausgehenden Satz Bezug genommen werden: „Auch die Schule hat ...".

Zu 5.: In Zeile 11 könnte man *local population* zunächst wörtlich mit „örtliche Bevölkerung" übersetzen und später dann in „die dort ansässige Bevölkerung/die Menschen, die dort leben" verbessern.

Zu 6.: Zu *help* (Zeile 13) könnte man folgende Varianten notieren: „helfen / behilflich sein / Unterstützung leisten / dazu beitragen"; wahrscheinlich würde wohl die letzte ausgewählt werden.

Vor der Übersetzung des folgenden Textes sollte man sich selbstverständlich auch noch einmal aller Übersetzungshilfen erinnern, die in den vorangegangenen Kapiteln dieses Kurses vermittelt wurden. Z. B. muß man bei den Zeilen 9, 10, 14 und 17 an die verschiedenen Wege, englische Passivsätze wiederzugeben, denken. Bei *(in the) country* (Zeilen 10 und 13) gilt es, die zum Kontext passenden Übersetzungsvarianten zu finden; bei *movement* (Zeile 11) ist auf die Möglichkeit, die Wortart zu verändern, zu achten, und *local* (Zeile 11) darf nicht mit dem im Deutschen ähnlichen Wort verwechselt werden.

A QUESTION OF CLASS

In spite of the fact that there are certain differences between British and American spelling and vocabulary, Standard English – the written English of books and newspapers – is much the same throughout the English-speaking world. The
5 newspapers of New York, Sydney, Dublin and London, for example, are all written in very similar English. But of course people do not all *speak* in the same way; they speak with an American accent, Irish accent, English accent, etc. Moreover, some people speak a dialect.
Today regional accents can be heard in all the big towns and cities of England;
10 dialects, on the other hand, are spoken mainly in the country, where there is less movement of the local population. But less and less people are speaking dialect now, since radio and TV have taken Standard English into practically every home in the country. Education has helped too.
One kind of speech that cannot be said to be typical of a particular region in
15 Britain is that of newsreaders on TV and radio, which has become known as BBC English. Unlike Standard English – which developed from a regional dialect – BBC English cannot be considered a regional accent. It is a social accent. Whether a person speaks BBC English is very much a question of what class he belongs to. The higher up the social ladder a person is, the more likely he is
20 to use it, and the less likely he is to show where he comes from by his speech. So BBC English is not the English of London; working-class Londoners have their own accent.

Hinweise
zur Benutzung eines englisch-deutschen Wörterbuchs

Wenn man sich über die Bedeutung eines englischen Wortes nicht im klaren ist und sie auch aus dem Zusammenhang nicht eindeutig erschließen kann, wird man ein Wörterbuch zu Rate ziehen.
Wörterbücher weichen in ihrer Gestaltung teilweise beträchtlich voneinander ab. Dennoch gibt es eine Reihe von Hinweisen, deren Beachtung die Benutzung aller Wörterbücher erleichtert und das Auffinden der gesuchten Wörter beschleunigt. Solche Hinweise sind hier zusammengestellt und werden in Verbindung mit dem Wörterbuchausschnitt auf der gegenüberliegenden Seite veranschaulicht. Im übrigen ist es in jedem Fall ratsam, sich mit den Erklärungen der Zeichen und Abkürzungen eines Wörterbuchs vertraut zu machen.

① Man schlägt das unbekannte Wort unter dem *Stichwort* nach. Dabei ist zu beachten, daß häufig eine Tilde (~) verwendet wird, um die Wiederholung eines Stichworts zu vermeiden.

② Man überprüft, ob das Stichwort nach *Wortarten* (Substantiv, Verb usw.) untergliedert ist.

③ Man stellt fest, ob unter der jeweiligen Wortart *Wörter mit verschiedenen Bedeutungen* zusammengefaßt sind.

④ Sind unterschiedliche Bedeutungen aufgeführt, muß man den *Zusammenhang* genauer betrachten, in dem das Wort im Text steht. Viele Wörterbücher kennzeichnen das Fachgebiet durch Symbole oder drucktechnische Mittel (z.B. Kursivschrift).

⑤ Da häufig mehrere *sinnverwandte Wörter* nebeneinander erscheinen, muß man sich für dasjenige Wort entscheiden, das am besten in den Zusammenhang paßt. Manchmal ist es sogar angebracht, ein sinnverwandtes Wort zu wählen, das nicht im Wörterbuch enthalten ist.

⑥ Bei *festen Fügungen* empfiehlt es sich, nicht nur unter einem Bestandteil, sondern unter allen wichtigen Elementen nachzuschlagen.

⑦ *Ableitungen* (z.B. chargeable, changeable) sind nicht immer als selbständige Stichwörter aufgeführt. Sie können auch unter dem Grundwort eingetragen sein.

① *Stichwort*
in halbfetter Schrift

① *Tilde*
anstelle des Stichworts

② *Römische Ziffern*
zur Unterscheidung
der Wortart

③ *Arabische Ziffern*
zur Bedeutungsunter-
scheidung

④ *Symbole/Kursivschrift*
zur Angabe des Fach-
gebiets

④ *Kursivschrift*
zur Erläuterung
der Bedeutung

charge [tʃɑːdʒ] **I.** *v/t.* **1.** belasten, beladen, beschweren (*with* mit) (*mst fig.*); **2.** *Batterie, Gewehr etc.* laden; **3.** (an)füllen; ⊕, ⚔ beschicken; ⌒ sättigen; **4.** beauftragen (*with* mit); ermahnen; einschärfen (*dat.*): *he was ~d with a delicate mission* ihm war e-e heikle Aufgabe übertragen *od.* anvertraut; *I ~d him not to forget* ich schärfte ihm ein, es nicht zu vergessen; **5.** Weisungen geben (*dat.*); belehren: *to ~ the jury* den Geschworenen Rechtsbelehrung geben; **6.** zur Last legen, vorwerfen (*on dat.*): *he ~d the fault on me* er schrieb mir die Schuld zu; **7.** beschuldigen, anklagen (*with gen.*): *to ~ s.o. with murder*; **8.** angreifen, anfallen; anstürmen gegen: *to ~ the enemy*; **9.** *Preis etc.* fordern, berechnen: *he ~d (me) a dollar for it* er berechnete (mir) e-n Dollar dafür; **10.** ✝ *j-n für od. mit et.* belasten, *j-m et.* in Rechnung stellen: *~ these goods to me* (*od. to my account*); **II.** *v/i.* **11.** angreifen; stürmen: *the lion ~d at me* der Löwe fiel mich an; **12.** (e-n Preis) fordern, (Kosten) berechnen: *to ~ too much* zuviel berechnen; *I shall not ~ for it* ich werde es nicht berechnen; **III.** *s.* **13.** ⚔, *mot.* Ladung *f*; ⊕ (Spreng)Ladung *f*; Füllung *f*, Beschickung *f*; *metall.* Einsatz *m*; **14.** Belastung *f*, Forderung *f* (*beide a.* ✝), Last *f*, Bürde *f*; Anforderung *f*, Beanspruchung *f*: *to be a ~ on s.o.* j-m zur Last fallen; *a first ~ on s.th.* e-e erste Forderung an et. (*acc.*); **15.** (*a. pl.*) Preis *m*, Kosten *pl.*, Unkosten *pl.*; Gebühr *f*: *no ~, free of ~* kostenlos, gratis; *to make a ~ for s.th.* et. an-, berechnen; **16.** Aufgabe *f*, Amt *n*, Pflicht *f*, Verantwortung *f*; **17.** Aufsicht *f*, Obhut *f*, Pflege *f*, Sorge *f*; Verwahrung *f*; Verwaltung *f*: *person in ~* Leiter, Verantwortliche(r); *to put s.o. in ~* j-m die Leitung übertragen; *to be in ~ of* vorstehen (*dat.*), verwalten (*acc.*), verantwortlich sein für, versorgen (*acc.*), betreuen (*acc.*); *under* (*od. in*) *the ~ in* der Obhut *od.* Pflege, unter der Aufsicht (*of gen.*); *to take ~* (*of*) die Verwaltung (*gen.*) *od.* Aufsicht (*über acc.*) *od.* Sorge (für j-n *od.* et.) übernehmen; **18.** Gewahrsam *m*: *to give s.o. in ~* j-n der Polizei übergeben; *to take s.o. in ~* j-n festnehmen; **19.** Mündel *m*; Pflegebefohlene(r *m*) *f*, Schützling *m*; **20.** Befehl *m*, Anweisung *f*, Mahnung *f*; ⚖ Rechtsbelehrung *f*; **21.** Vorwurf *m*, Beschuldigung *f*; ⚖ (Punkt *m* der) Anklage *f*: *on a ~ of murder* wegen Mord; *to return to the ~ fig.* auf das alte Thema zurückkommen; **22.** Angriff *m*, (An)Sturm *m*.

char·gé ['ʃɑːʒeɪ] *abbr.* für *chargé d'affaires.*

charge·a·ble ['tʃɑːdʒəbl] *adj.* □ **1.** anzurechnen(d), zu Lasten gehen(d) (*to* von); zu berechnen(d) (*on dat.*); zu belasten(d) (*with* mit); *teleph.* gebührenpflichtig; **2.** zahlbar; **3.** strafbar.

● *Abkürzung für die* Wortart ②

● *Abkürzung für das* Fachgebiet ④

● *Wörter mit verwandten Bedeutungen* ⑤

● *Feste Fügungen* ⑥

● *Hinweis auf übertragene Bedeutung* ④

● *Ableitung* ⑦

Notes on the authors in Unit 4

E. E. Cummings (1894 – 1962), born in Cambridge, Mass. Began writing poetry at Harvard University. Became a full-time writer and painter after World War I. Wrote many books of poetry, a few plays and other works.

W. H. Davies (1871 – 1940), born in Newport, near Cardiff. Made repeated visits to the U.S.A., travelling around as a tramp and street singer. Published several works of fiction and collections of poems.

Robert Frost (1874 – 1963), born in San Francisco but spent most of his life in New England (the six north-eastern states of the U.S.A.). Started writing as a teenager, but achieved his first real success with poems published during a stay in Britain, 1912 – 1915. Won the Pulitzer prize for poetry four times.

Ernest Hemingway (1899 – 1961), born in Oak Park, Ill. Became a reporter at 18 for the "Kansas City Star". Got badly wounded in Italy during World War I. Travelled through Europe and the Middle East, working as a journalist and writing short stories and novels. Was also influenced by his experiences in the Spanish Civil War and World War II as well as in Cuba and Africa. Won the Pulitzer prize in 1953 and the Nobel prize for literature in 1954.

Adrian Henri (1932 –), born in Birkenhead, near Liverpool. Studied art at Durham University. Worked as a painter and teacher. In 1967 formed the poetry/rock group "Liverpool Scene". Now a full-time writer and performer of his work, with and without music.

Roger McGough (1937 –), born in Liverpool, the son of a docker. Studied French and geography at Hull University, taught for three years, then became a member of a pop group, "The Scaffold". Has written poems, plays and a novel.

E. V. Milner (? – ?), contributed a lot of poetry to the London magazine "Punch" in the 1950s, writing from an address in Lincolnshire. Strangely, always refused to provide any information about himself (or *her*self). According to "Punch", trying to find out more about Milner's identity "was an office game at one time, as he had become such a man of mystery".

William F. Nolan (1928 –), born in Kansas City. Editor and science fiction reviewer for the "Los Angeles Times". Has won the E. A. Poe prize for Mystery Writers (twice) as well as prizes for science fiction films and TV films.

John O'Hara (1905 – 1970), born in Pottsville, Pa., the oldest of eight children. Worked as an engineer, ship's steward, factory worker, farm worker, cinema agent and reporter before publishing his first novel in 1934 and becoming famous. The author of many novels, plays and short stories.

Brian Patten (1946 –), born in Liverpool. Has had poems published in many magazines and collections of poetry. Has also written children's books and modern fables.

James Thurber (1894 – 1961), born in Columbus, Ohio. Worked as a journalist in Columbus, Paris and New York before joining the "New Yorker" magazine in 1927. Became famous both as a writer and as a comic artist.

Names

Boys' names

Adrian [ˈeɪdrɪən]
Albert [ˈælbət]
Andrew [ˈændruː]
Austin [ˈɒstɪn]
Calvin [ˈkælvɪn]
Cyril [ˈsɪrəl]
Ernest [ˈɜːnɪst]
Humphrey [ˈhʌmfrɪ]
Jeremy [ˈdʒerəmɪ]
Malcolm [ˈmælkəm]

Girls' names

Caroline [ˈkærəlaɪn]
Hilary [ˈhɪlərɪ]
Lisa [ˈliːzɑː, ˈlaɪzə]
Marilyn [ˈmærɪlɪn]
Nancy [ˈnænsɪ]
Pauline
 [ˈpɔːliːn, pɔːˈliːn]
Vanessa [vəˈnesə]

Surnames

Baines [beɪnz]
Bancroft [ˈbænkrɒft]
Beckett [ˈbekɪt]
Benyon [ˈbenjən]
Bishop [ˈbɪʃəp]
Blair [bleə]
Bright [braɪt]
Caxton [ˈkækstən]
Coolidge [ˈkuːlɪdʒ]
Costain [kɒˈsteɪn]
Crosland [ˈkrɒslənd]
Cummings [ˈkʌmɪŋz]
Darley [ˈdɑːlɪ]
De Freitas
 [dəˈfreɪtəs]
Drevitts [ˈdrevɪts]
Dylan [ˈdɪlən]
Frost [frɒst]
Harkness [ˈhɑːknɪs]

Harvard [ˈhɑːvəd]
Hemingway [ˈhemɪŋweɪ]
Henri [ˈhenrɪ]
Holmes [həʊmz]
Hughes [hjuːz]
Kinnock [ˈkɪnək]
McAllister [məˈkælɪstə]
McEldowney
 [ˈmækldaʊnɪ]
McElrea [məˈkelreɪ]
McGough [məˈgɒf]
Mikes [ˈmiːkeʃ]
Mitchell [ˈmɪtʃl]
Moore [mʊə]
Muggeridge [ˈmʌgərɪdʒ]
Murdock [ˈmɜːdɒk]
Nolan [ˈnəʊlən]
O'Hara [əʊˈhɑːrə]
Partington-Holmes
 [ˈpɑːtɪŋtənˈhəʊmz]
Patten [ˈpætn]
Ruskin [ˈrʌskɪn]
Schlesinger
 [ˈslezɪndʒə]
Skinner [ˈskɪnə]
Stanton [ˈstæntən]
Thatcher [ˈθætʃə]
Thorn [θɔːn]
Thurber [ˈθɜːbə]
Van Ness [ˈ-ˈ-]
Vaughan [vɔːn]

Place names

Aberdeen [æbəˈdiːn]
Austria [ˈɒstrɪə]
Bangladesh [bæŋgləˈdeʃ]
Bedwellty [bedˈweltɪ]
Bengal [beŋˈgɔːl]
Bolsover [ˈbəʊlzəʊvə]
Brazil [brəˈzɪl]
the British Isles
 [ˈbrɪtɪʃˈaɪlz]
Chichester [ˈtʃɪtʃɪstə]
Denmark [ˈdenmɑːk]
Egypt [ˈiːdʒɪpt]

Grimsby [ˈgrɪmzbɪ]
Herefordshire
 [ˈherɪfədʃə]
Huddersfield
 [ˈhʌdəsfiːld]
Hythe [haɪð]
Iceland [ˈaɪslənd]
Iran [ɪˈrɑːn]
Korea [kəˈrɪə]
Lancaster [ˈlæŋkəstə]
Libya [ˈlɪbɪə]
Malaysia [məˈleɪzɪə]
Nigeria [naɪˈdʒɪərɪə]
New Guinea
 [njuːˈgɪnɪ]
Norway [ˈnɔːweɪ]
Pontypool [pɒntɪˈpuːl]
Portugal [ˈpɔːtʃʊgl]
Reading [ˈredɪŋ]
Rhodesia [rəʊˈdiːʒə]
Rochdale [ˈrɒtʃdeɪl]
Saudi Arabia
 [ˈsaʊdɪəˈreɪbɪə]
Singapore [sɪŋgəˈpɔː]
Spain [speɪn]
St. Malo [sənˈmɑːləʊ]
Sweden [ˈswiːdn]
Sydney [ˈsɪdnɪ]
Thayerville [ˈθeɪəvɪl]
U.S.S.R. [juːesesˈɑː]
West Point [ˈ-ˈ-]
Woolton [ˈwʊltən]
Worcester [ˈwʊstə]
Zambia [ˈzæmbɪə]

Other names

British Leyland
 [ˈleɪlənd]
Elite [eɪˈliːt]
Esperanto [espəˈræntəʊ]
Metro-Goldwyn-Mayer
 [ˈmetrəʊˈgəʊldwɪnˈmeɪə]
Nobel [nəʊˈbel, ˈnəʊbel]
Pulitzer [ˈpjuːlɪtsə]
Scaffold [ˈskæfəld]

119

Irregular verbs

Simple present	Simple past	Present perfect
I'm, you're, he's	I was, you were	I've been, he's been
I beat	I beat	I've beaten
I become	I became	I've become
I begin	I began	I've begun
I bet	I bet	I've bet
I bite	I bit	I've bitten
I blow	I blew [u:]	I've blown
I break [eɪ]	I broke	I've broken
I bring	I brought [ɔ:]	I've brought
I broadcast [ɑ:]	I broadcast	I've broadcast
I build	I built	I've built
it bursts [ɜ:]	it burst	it's burst
I buy	I bought [ɔ:]	I've bought
I catch	I caught [ɔ:]	I've caught
I choose [u:]	I chose [əʊ]	I've chosen
I cling	I clung [ʌ]	I've clung
I come	I came	I've come
it costs	it cost	it's cost
I creep	I crept	I've crept
I cut	I cut	I've cut
I deal [i:]	I dealt [e]	I've dealt
I dig	I dug [ʌ]	I've dug
I do [u:], he does [ʌ]	I did	I've done [ʌ]
I draw	I drew [u:]	I've drawn
I dream	I dreamt [e]	I've dreamt
I drink	I drank	I've drunk
I drive	I drove	I've driven [ɪ]
I eat	I ate [e]	I've eaten
I fall	I fell	I've fallen
I feed	I fed	I've fed
I feel	I felt	I've felt
I fight	I fought [ɔ:]	I've fought
I find	I found	I've found
I fly	I flew [u:]	I've flown [əʊ]
I forget	I forgot	I've forgotten
I freeze	I froze	I've frozen
I get	I got	I've got
I give	I gave	I've given
I go	I went	I've gone [ɒ]
I grow	I grew [u:]	I've grown
I have, he has; I've got	I had	I've had
I hang	I hung	I've hung
I hear [ɪə]	I heard [ɜ:]	I've heard
I hide	I hid	I've hidden
I hit	I hit	I've hit
I hold	I held	I've held
I hurt [ɜ:]	I hurt	I've hurt
I keep	I kept	I've kept
I know	I knew [ju:]	I've known
I lay	I laid [eɪ]	I've laid
I lead	I led	I've led
I lean [i:]	I leant [e]	I've leant
I leave	I left	I've left

Simple present	Simple past	Present perfect
I lend	I lent	I've lent
I let	I let	I've let
I lie	I lay [eɪ]	I've lain [eɪ]
I light	I lit	I've lit
I lose [uː]	I lost [ɒ]	I've lost
I make	I made	I've made
I mean	I meant [e]	I've meant
I meet	I met	I've met
I pay	I paid [eɪ]	I've paid
I put [ʊ]	I put	I've put
I quit	I quit	I've quit
I read	I read [e]	I've read [e]
I ride	I rode	I've ridden
I ring	I rang	I've rung
it rises	it rose	it's risen [ɪ]
I run	I ran	I've run
I say	I said [e]	I've said
I see	I saw	I've seen
I sell	I sold	I've sold
I send	I sent	I've sent
I set off	I set off	I've set off
I sew [əʊ]	I sewed	I've sewn
I shake	I shook [ʊ]	I've shaken
it shines	it shone [ɒ]	it's shone
I shoot	I shot	I've shot
I show	I showed	I've shown
I shut	I shut	I've shut
I sing	I sang	I've sung
I sink	I sank	I've sunk
I sit	I sat	I've sat
I sleep	I slept	I've slept
I slide	I slid	I've slid
I speak	I spoke	I've spoken
I spend	I spent	I've spent
I spit	I spat	I've spat
I spread [e]	I spread	I've spread
I stand	I stood [ʊ]	I've stood
I steal	I stole	I've stolen
I stick	I stuck	I've stuck
it stinks	it stank	it's stunk
it strikes	it struck	it's struck
I swim	I swam	I've swum
I swing	I swung	I've swung
I take	I took [ʊ]	I've taken
I teach	I taught [ɔː]	I've taught
I tear [eə]	I tore	I've torn
I tell	I told	I've told
I think	I thought [ɔː]	I've thought
I throw	I threw [uː]	I've thrown
I wake up	I woke up	I've woken up
I wear [eə]	I wore	I've worn
I win	I won [ʌ]	I've won
I write	I wrote	I've written

Phrasal verbs (see also p. 47)

This is a complete list of phrasal verbs you've learned so far. The German equivalents are intended as a help only – the actual translation will often depend on the context.

beat up ['-'-]	zusammenschlagen	make up	sich ausdenken
blow out	ausblasen	mess up	durcheinanderbringen
breathe in	einatmen	move on	weitergehen, fortfahren
breathe out	ausatmen	move up	aufrücken
build up	aufbauen; sich entwickeln		
		pick up	aufheben; mitbekommen
		point out	hinweisen auf
call in	vorbeikommen	put away	wegräumen
call out	ausrufen	put on	anziehen
calm down	(sich) beruhigen	put through	durchstellen
check in	sich anmelden, abfertigen lassen	put up	aufstellen; erhöhen
cheer up	aufheitern	queue up	sich anstellen
clear up	aufräumen; sich aufklären		
		ring up	anrufen
come back	zurückkommen	run out	ausgehen, zu Ende gehen
come in	hereinkommen		
come up	herankommen	set off	aufbrechen
		settle in	sich einleben
dry up	abtrocknen	sit down	sich setzen
		speak up	lauter sprechen
fall over	hinfallen	stand up	aufstehen
fatten up	mästen	start off	beginnen
fill in/out	ausfüllen	stay down	sitzenbleiben
fill up	(auf-)füllen	stay up	aufbleiben
find out	herausfinden	strip off	abziehen
		switch off	ab-, ausschalten
get ahead	vorankommen	switch on	einschalten
get away	entkommen		
get up	aufstehen	take down	abnehmen
give away	weggeben, verschenken	take off	ausziehen; starten; (sich) freinehmen
give back	zurückgeben	take out	herausnehmen; ausführen
give up	aufgeben	take over	übernehmen
go away	weggehen	tear up	zerreißen
go back	zurückgehen	turn down	leiser stellen; ablehnen
go off	fortgehen; losgehen	turn off	ab-, ausschalten; anöden
go on	weitergehen, fortfahren	turn on	einschalten; begeistern
go out	ausgehen	turn over	umblättern, -drehen
go up	steigen	turn round	sich umdrehen
grow up	auf-, heranwachsen	turn up	lauter stellen
keep up	beibehalten	wake up	aufwachen
knock down	abreißen	wash up	abwaschen
		work out	ausrechnen, -arbeiten
leave out	aus-, weglassen	write down	auf-, niederschreiben
look up	nachschlagen		

English words and phrases

1 A	petition [pɪ'tɪʃn]	a written request or protest, signed by a lot of people	Bittschrift, Eingabe, Gesuch
	power ['paʊə]	The engine wasn't powerful enough to pull 30 carriages. It hadn't got enough *power*. The U.S.A. is a super-*power*. Customs officers have got the *power* to arrest people for smuggling.	Kraft, Macht, Gewalt; Befugnis
	nuclear ['nju:klɪə]	Two *nuclear* bombs fell on Japan in 1945.	Atom-, Kern-
	nuclear power station ['--'----]	a *nuclear power station* 	Kernkraftwerk
	taxpayer ['---]	somebody who pays tax	Steuerzahler(in)
	defence [dɪ'fens]	The school's football team can defend well. It's got a good *defence*.	Verteidigung
	pension ['penʃn]	Mr Hill, 65, doesn't work any more. He gets a *pension* of £20 per week from the government.	Rente, Pension
	affect [ə'fekt]	have an effect on Alcoholic drinks *affect* people's driving.	betreffen; sich auswirken auf
	federal ['fedrəl]	Each U.S. state has got a separate government. There's also a *federal* government (in Washington, D.C.) for the whole country.	Bundes-
	republic [rɪ'pʌblɪk]	similar to the German word	Republik
	monarchy ['mɒnəkɪ]	a country with a king or queen	Monarchie
	parliament ['pɑ:ləmənt]		Parlament
	Houses of Parliament	There's a picture of the *Houses of Parliament* on page 11 of this book.	Parlamentsgebäude in London
	(House of) Commons ['kɒmənz]		Unterhaus
	lord [lɔ:d]	Isn't there a statue of a *lord* in Trafalgar Square? – Yes. It's *Lord* Nelson.	Adliger, Lord
	(House of) Lords		Oberhaus
	elect [ɪ'lekt]	As a result of the election Dennis became president. He was *elected* (president).	wählen (zum, zur)
	voter ['vəʊtə]	In the recent election 200 *voters* gave their *votes* to Dennis, so he was elected.	Wähler
	vote (n.) [vəʊt]		(Wahl-)Stimme
	inherit [ɪn'herɪt]	On Bill's death Liz *inherited* £1,000,000.	erben
	title ['taɪtl]	similar to the German word	Titel
	appoint [ə'pɔɪnt]	The President *appointed* a new Secretary of the Interior. But Al wasn't *appointed* Secretary of the Interior. He wasn't *appointed* to the job.	ernennen, berufen
	bill	a draft for a new law	Gesetzesvorlage
	turn down ['-'-]	reject (a plan, suggestion, etc.)	ablehnen, -weisen
	insist on [ɪn'sɪst]	demand with emphasis	darauf bestehen, daß
	minister ['mɪnɪstə]	a government official, e.g. the *Minister* of Defence, the *Minister* for Europe	Minister(in)
	Prime Minister [praɪm'mɪnɪstə]	the head of the (British) government (short form: PM)	Premierminister, -(in), Ministerpräsident(in)
	Cabinet ['kæbɪnət]	a council of top ministers who help the PM to decide government policy	Kabinett
	party	a political organization	Partei
	opposition [ɒpə'zɪʃn]	We use the same word in German.	Opposition
	civil servant [sɪvl'sɜ:vənt]	an official employed permanently by the government	Regierungsbeamter, -beamtin

Unit 1

Acquisition

moreover [mɔːˈrəʊvə]	a rather formal word for "in addition", "besides", "also", "what's more" This hat is nice and, *moreover,* it's cheap.	ferner, überdies
turn (to/into)	Jerry's face went white. It *turned* white. Heat *turns* ice *(in)to* water.	werden (zu), (sich) verwandeln (in)
politician [pɒləˈtɪʃn]	somebody whose job is politics	Politiker(in)
Member of Parliament	one of the 635 politicians in the House of Commons (short form: MP)	Abgeordnete(r) des Unterhauses
represent [reprɪˈzent]	The boss couldn't attend the meeting, so his assistant *represented* him there. This drawing *represents* a girl.	vertreten; darstellen

Westminster [ˈwesmɪnstə]	an area of London; another name for "the Houses of Parliament"	Westminster
constituency [kənˈstɪtjʊənsɪ]	one of the 635 areas of the U.K. which each elect 1 MP to the House of Commons	Wahlbezirk
constituent	a voter living in a particular constituency	Wähler (eines Wahlbezirks)
Am I supposed to come? [səˈpəʊzd]	Do you/they expect me to come? That was a joke. You're *supposed to* laugh! Homework *isn't supposed to* be done in class.	Soll ich kommen?/ Erwartet man, daß ich komme?
general election	an election at which all 635 constituencies elect an MP on the same day	allgemeine Parlamentswahlen
by-election [ˈ----]	an election in an individual constituency that takes place between general elections	Nachwahl
Foreign Secretary [ˈ--ˈ---]	the minister responsible for foreign affairs	Außenminister(in)
announce [əˈnaʊns]	give an item of news in an official way At the party Graham and Julie *announced* that they would marry in April.	bekanntgeben, -machen
candidate [ˈkændɪdət]	somebody trying to pass an examination, be elected or be chosen for a job	Kandidat(in), Bewerber(in)
Labour (adj., adv., n.) [ˈleɪbə]	The *Labour* Party, the *Liberal* Party, and the *Conservative* Party are 3 important parties in the U.K. Joe votes *Liberal* or *Conservative;* he votes for the *Liberals* or for the *Conservatives.* Sue votes *Labour;* she votes for the *Labour* Party.	Labour-, Arbeiter-; Labour Party
Liberal (adj., adv., n.) [ˈlɪbrəl]		liberal; Liberale(r)
Conservative (adj., adv., n.) [kənˈsɜːvətɪv]		konservativ; Konservative(r)
Tory [ˈtɔːrɪ]	a colloquial word for "Conservative"	Tory
democratic [deməˈkrætɪk]	similar to the German word	demokratisch
socialism [ˈsəʊʃəlɪzm]	similar to the German word	Sozialismus
socialist (adj., n.) [ˈsəʊʃəlɪst]	similar to the German word (sometimes used to describe members of the Labour Party)	sozialistisch; Sozialist(in)
Independent Democratic Labour	a small political party in Britain	Unabh. Demokr. Arbeiterpartei
interviewer [ˈ----]	somebody who interviews people	Interviewer(in)
Common Market [--ˈ--]	Britain became a member of the *Common Market* in 1973.	Europäische Gemeinschaft, EG
profit [ˈprɒfɪt]	Al makes a *profit* of £110 on every car he sells.	Gewinn, Profit
(trade) union [ˈtreɪdˈjuːnjən]	an organization of workers in a certain industry or trade which tries to improve conditions and protect workers' interests	Gewerkschaft

Acquisition

Unit 1

scientist ['saɪəntɪst]	somebody who works in the field of science	(Natur-)Wissenschaftler(in)
idiotic [ɪdɪ'ɒtɪk]	similar to the German word	idiotisch
campaign (n.) [kæm'peɪn]	Thomas supports a *campaign* against nuclear bombs. Helga, his wife, does this, too. She also	Kampagne, Kampf
campaign (v.)	*campaigns* for women's rights.	sich einsetzen, werben
buyer	somebody whose job it is to buy things for a firm (usually in large amounts)	Einkäufer(in)
frozen food ['--'-]		Tiefkühlkost
trawler ['trɔ:lə]	This kind of fishing-boat is a *trawler*.	Fischtrawler
discipline ['dɪsɪplɪn]	similar to the German word	Disziplin; Schulung
agent ['eɪdʒənt]	Some writers pay an *agent* to find someone who will publish their books. Some MPs have got a political *agent*. A foreign *agent* stole the new plans.	Agent, Vermittler, Bevollmächtigter
leaflet ['li:flət]		Flug-, Merkblatt
key	most important Valerie plays a *key* role in the organization.	Haupt-, Schlüssel-
issue ['ɪʃu:]	matter, topic, affair, problem	(Streit-)Frage
conference ['kɒnfrəns]	We use almost the same word in German.	Konferenz
be willing to ['wɪlɪŋ]	Will you help? *Are* you *willing to* (help)?	bereit sein (zu)
shake hands (with)	When the President was introduced to the PM, they *shook hands*. – But the PM forgot to *shake hands* with the President's wife.	die Hand geben
shopper ['ʃɒpə]	somebody who goes shopping	Käufer(in)
report	make a report (about)	berichten
canvass ['kænvəs]	visit people during an election campaign, asking them to vote for a certain party	um (Stimmen) werben
sticker ['stɪkə]	some *stickers*	Aufkleber
Abe **got** shot.	Abe was shot. Tony was delighted when he *got* promoted.	Abe wurde erschossen.
seat	(here:) a place in the House of Commons	Sitz, Mandat
Proportional Representation [prə'pɔ:ʃənl reprɪzen'teɪʃn]	an election system (like the one used in the Federal Republic of Germany)	Verhältniswahlrecht
happen to do something	Steve and Lucy didn't plan to meet at the station. They just *happened to* meet there. They both *happened to* be going to London. Do you *happen to* know what's on TV tonight?	etwas zufällig tun
Pete **may** be late.	Pete might be late. Those clouds are dark. It *may* rain soon.	Pete wird vielleicht zu spät kommen.
You**'re to** come home early.	You mustn't come home late. Mother says you've got to stay at home. You *aren't to* go out. Do you understand?	Du sollst rechtzeitig nach Hause kommen.
The firm **is to** be sold.	It has been arranged. The firm will be sold. Hundreds of workers *are to* lose their jobs.	Die Firma wird verkauft.
keep ... ing (s.th.)	go on ... ing (s.th.) The new waiter *kept* break*ing* things. We'll stay at home if it *keeps* rain*ing*.	(etwas) immer wieder oder weiter(hin) tun

125

Unit 1

Acquisition

put up with [-'--]	Barbara's radio was too loud. Her father turned it off. He couldn't stand the noise. He refused to *put up with* it.	aushalten, ruhig hinnehmen, sich gefallen lassen
(opinion) poll [ə'pɪnjən'pəʊl]	a survey of people's views on a particular topic. The *(opinion) poll* showed Blair in the lead.	Meinungsumfrage
(un-)likely ['laɪklɪ] It's **likely/unlikely** to rain.	Will Sandra be late? – It's very *likely*. She's *likely* to be late. Will Lisa win the race? – It's *unlikely*. She's *unlikely* to win.	(un-)wahrscheinlich Es wird wahrscheinlich/wahrscheinlich nicht regnen.
invest [ɪn'vest]	Bert has *invested* £50 in a company that builds windmills.	investieren, anlegen
network ['--]	a complex system, e.g. of roads, railways	Netz
accuse s.b. **of** (s.th.) [ə'kju:z]	claim that s.b. has done s.th. bad or wrong. The policeman *accused* Marcia *of* stealing a blouse. She was *accused of* this.	jn. (einer Sache) beschuldigen, anklagen
importance [ɪm'pɔ:təns]	the quality of being important	Wichtigkeit
opponent [ə'pəʊnənt]	somebody who's against something. Mike is an *opponent* of apartheid.	Gegner(in)
I/we shall, shan't [ʃæl, ʃəl, ʃɑ:nt]	a more formal way of saying "I/we will, won't". We *shall* arrive at 7. We *shan't* be late.	Ich/wir werde(n), werde(n) nicht
bribery ['braɪbərɪ]	offering money or a present to s.b. in order to influence or persuade the person (often to do s.th. that's illegal)	Bestechung
manipulation [mənɪpjʊ'leɪʃn]	arranging or controlling things in a way that's clever but not fair or honest	Manipulation, Machenschaft
polling day ['pəʊlɪŋdeɪ]	the day when an election is held	Wahltag
polling station ['----]	a building where people vote on polling day	Wahllokal
no sooner ... than	another expression for "hardly ... when". The meeting began as soon as Liz arrived. Liz had *no sooner* arrived *than* the meeting began.	kaum ..., als
favourite (n.)	similar to the German word	Favorit(in), (Publikums-) Günstling
be obliged to [ə'blaɪdʒd]	should, have to (because of a promise, duty, etc.). The traffic lights turned red. So Louise *was obliged to* stop the car.	müssen, (dazu) verpflichtet sein, sollen
obligation [ɒblɪ'geɪʃn]	Martin is obliged to attend the meeting. He's got an *obligation* to the company. When an accident happens, everyone is under an *obligation* to help.	Verpflichtung
recount ['ri:'kaʊnt]	Count your money again. *Recount* it.	noch einmal zählen
take a seat	sit down	Platz nehmen
(in-)effective [ɪ'fektɪv]	(not) useful, helpful, having an effect. This medicine is *effective* against the flu.	(un-)wirksam

1 T
detailed ['di:teɪld]	with a lot of details	ausführlich
public school ['--'-]	a private school (usually a boarding school), where pupils pay fees; not a school that's paid for by the government from taxes	"Public School", (Privatschule, meist mit Internat
banker	somebody who owns a bank, or is a senior worker or a partner in a bank	Bankier, Bankdirektor
record ['rekɔ:d]	what's written down or known about the past of somebody or something. Oliver has got a long *record* as a thief. A diary is a *record* of daily events.	Geschichte, Protokoll; Leumund, Ruf

Text | | | Unit 1

coal [kəʊl]	Put some more *coal* on the fire, please.	Kohle(n)
mine	Ian works underground in a gold-*mine*.	Bergwerk, Mine
miner ['maɪnə]	George works in a coal-mine. He's a coal-*miner*.	Bergarbeiter, Bergmann
cycling ['saɪklɪŋ]	riding a bike	Radeln, Radfahren
partly	Liz goes to the disco *partly* for the music and *partly* to meet all her friends.	teils, zum Teil, teilweise
penal reform ['pi:nəlrɪ'fɔ:m]	improving the way people are dealt with after they've committed crimes	Strafrechtsreform
unlike ['-'-]	not the same as, in contrast to Rachel is *unlike* her cousin. *Unlike* him she's very shy. He's not shy at all.	anders als, im Gegensatz zu
sponsor (v.)	act as a sponsor for	(finanziell) unterstützen
conscience ['kɒnʃəns]	Tony apologized to Chris. He had a bad *conscience* about a letter he'd written her. It had been on his *conscience* all week.	Gewissen
judgement ['dʒʌdʒmənt]	Nick has become a millionaire. Rosemary showed good *judgement* in marrying him.	Urteil(svermögen), Beurteilung, Ermessen
conflict (n.) ['kɒnflɪkt]	There's a *conflict* of opinion about the reasons for the *conflict* in Northern Ireland.	Konflikt, Streit, Widerspruch
conflict (v.) [kən'flɪkt]	Kathy disagrees with Ray. Her views *conflict* with his. They hold *conflicting* views.	im Gegensatz/Widerspruch stehen (zu)
backbencher ['bæk'bentʃə]	an MP who's not a minister or a leading member of his party, and so sits on one of the back seats in the House of Commons	Hinterbänkler, wenig einflußreicher Parlamentarier
pressure group ['--'-]	an organization of people, e.g. farmers or car-makers, who campaign to protect their interests, hoping to affect the decisions of MPs, local government, etc.	Interessenverband
committee [kə'mɪtɪ]	a group of people given a special job, e.g. examining a bill, running a club	Ausschuß, Komitee
judge	Everyone in the court stood up at once when the *judge* came into the room.	Richter(in)
debate [dɪ'beɪt]	After discussing the new bill in a long *debate*, most MPs voted in favour of it.	Verhandlung, Debatte
research (into/on) [rɪ'sɜ:tʃ]	Dr Fox, the animal expert, is doing some *research on* cats/*into* the habits of cats.	(Nach-)Forschung(en) (über)
library ['laɪbrərɪ]	a place where books can be borrowed or read	Bibliothek
line your pockets	The president has been accused of *lining his pockets* with the taxpayers' money.	sich die Taschen füllen
(in-)adequate ['ædɪkwət]	(not) enough, satisfactory Benjamin can't afford to get married. His pay isn't *adequate* to start a family.	(nicht) genug, genügend, ausreichend, angemessen
(company) director	someone who runs or helps to run a firm Paul Webb is a *director* of WEBB & FOOT Ltd. and also of OLD, COBB & WEBB Ltd.	Geschäftsführer, Aufsichtsratsmitglied
attractive [ə'træktɪv]	Elizabeth is pretty. She's very *attractive*. The trip Ellen is planning sounds *attractive*. The low prices at that shop are so *attractive* that everyone goes shopping there.	anziehend, reizvoll, verlockend
working-class (adj., n.) ['--'-]	Alec Murphy is a member of the *working-class*. He lives in a *working-class* area.	Arbeiterklasse; Arbeiter-

127

Unit 1   Text

bureaucracy [bjʊˈrɒkrəsɪ]	We use a similar word in German, e.g. to describe civil servants doing their duties according to rules but without considering people.	Bürokratie
circumstances [ˈsɜːkəmstænsɪz]	Before making up his mind, the judge listened to all the *circumstances* of the case. Ed had no choice under/in the *circumstances*.	Umstände, Verhältnisse, Bedingungen

1 Ex **ballot paper** [ˈbælət] a piece of paper on which you mark the candidate(s) or party you prefer — Wahlzettel
ballot box — Wahlurne
cross ✗ ✚ ✛ some *crosses* — Kreuz

cassette [kəˈset] a 60-minute *cassette* — Kassette
cassette recorder a *cassette recorder* — Kassettenrecorder
laundry [ˈlɔːndrɪ] a firm that washes clothes — Wäscherei
phrasal verb [ˈfreɪzl] "Come" is a simple verb. "Come on, come up, come in, come across" are *phrasal verbs*. — feste Verb-Adverb-Verbindung
psychiatrist [saɪˈkaɪətrɪst] a doctor who specializes in patients with problems of the mind — Psychiater
get the picture a colloquial expression meaning "understand" — begreifen, „kapieren"
the French French people, people born in France — (die) Franzosen
paraphrase [ˈpærəfreɪz] express in a different way — umschreiben
lawn-mower [ˈlɔːnməʊə] — Rasenmäher
fertilizer [ˈfɜːtəlaɪzə] — Düngemittel
immersion heater [ɪˈmɜːʃnhiːtə] — Tauchsieder
widow [ˈwɪdəʊ] — Witwe
How can/shall I put it? — Wie soll ich (es) sagen?
reproach s.b. **for** [rɪˈprəʊtʃ] criticize somebody for (bad behaviour, forgetting things, etc.) — jm. (etwas) vorwerfen, jn. tadeln
reproach (n.) The coach told Christine she hadn't tried hard enough. His *reproach* was justified. — Vorwurf, Tadel
lend, I lent, I've lent Dave borrowed Liz's tennis racket. She *lent* it to him for the afternoon. — (ver-, aus-)leihen
know better (than to) be sensible enough (not to) No gloves on such a cold day? You ought to *know better*. You ought to *know better than to* go out without gloves on such a cold day. — zu vernünftig sein (um zu), vernünftig genug sein (um nicht zu)
above (adj.) The description is given above. For further details look at the *above* description. — oben gegebener, -e
blame (n.) [bleɪm] Anne wasn't responsible for the accident, so she refused to take the *blame* for it. — Schuld, Tadel, Verantwortung
blame s.b. (for) give somebody the blame (for) The minister is responsible for this plan. If it doesn't work, *blame* him for it. — jn. verantwortlich machen (für), beschuldigen
mess up Your room is in a mess. Why don't you tidy it? – Because I'd soon *mess* it *up* again. — durcheinanderbringen, unordentlich machen
Look (here). *Look here,* that's not allowed. Stop it! — Hören Sie mal (zu)
I can't help it if ... It wasn't Nick's fault. He *couldn't help it if* the boat sank. — Ich kann es nicht ändern,/nichts dafür, daß ...

Exercises

Unit 1

traveller ['trævlə]	a person on a journey	Reisende(r)
traveller's cheque	a special kind of cheque that can be used in several countries	Reisescheck
get/be drunk	If Peter drinks even more wine, he'll *get drunk*. – I think he*'s drunk* already.	sich betrinken/ betrunken sein
1 S sense of duty	The captain was the last to leave the sinking ship because of his *sense of duty*.	Pflichtbewußsein

Unit 2

2 A Mandarin ['mændərɪn]	the language spoken by educated speakers in all parts of China	Hochchinesisch, Mandarin
Hindi ['hɪndɪ]	one of the official languages in India	Hindi
Urdu ['ʊədu:]	a form of Hindi that's used in Pakistan	Urdu
Arabic ['ærəbɪk]	the language spoken in Egypt, Libya, etc.	Arabisch
Portuguese [pɔ:tjʊ'gi:z]	the language spoken in Portugal and Brazil	Portugiesisch
Bengali [beŋ'gɔ:lɪ]	the language of Bengal	Bengalisch
Japanese [dʒæpə'ni:z]	referring to Japan; a citizen of Japan	japanisch; Japaner(in)
native language		Muttersprache
second language		Zweitsprache
knowledge ['nɒlɪdʒ]	Lisa knows a lot of English. Her *knowledge* of English is excellent. Liz married without her parents' *knowledge*.	Kenntnis(se), Wissen
yet (conj.)	but at the same time, however Anne's work is good, *yet* it could be better.	aber, (je-)doch, dennoch
airways ['- -]	another word for "airline"	Fluggesellschaft
Korean [kə'rɪən]	referring to Korea	koreanisch
Malaysian [mə'leɪzɪən]	referring to Malaysia	malaysisch
Scandinavian [skændɪ'neɪvjən]	referring to Norway, Sweden, Denmark and Iceland	skandinavisch
Swiss [swɪs]	referring to Switzerland	schweizerisch
status ['steɪtəs]	position in society, in a group, etc.; prestige The director's office is the biggest. It's a symbol of his *status* in the company.	Stellung, Rang; Prestige
1 in 5 own a car.	20% of the people own a car. Jean enjoys *1 in* 10 of the films she sees.	Jeder 5. besitzt einen Pkw.
remarkable [rɪ'mɑ:kəbl]	unusual, amazing, wonderful That pupil has made *remarkable* progress. His maths was *remarkably* bad last year.	ungewöhnlich, bemerkenswert, beachtlich
grow in	Since the new factory was built, the village has *grown in* size and importance.	zunehmen an
world-wide	Max's restaurant is famous throughout the world. It's got a *world-wide* reputation.	weltweit
last but not least	Sally enjoyed the concert. Her ticket was free, she had a good seat and, *last but not least,* the orchestra played well.	nicht zuletzt, nicht zu vergessen
culture ['kʌltʃə]	similar to the German word	Kultur
gradual(ly) ['grædʒʊəl]	slow and steady There's a *gradual* trend towards small cars. *Gradually* the baby learned how to talk.	allmählich

Unit 2   Acquisition

NATO ['neɪtəʊ]		(die) NATO
take over	An American firm bought Joe's company and *took over* his customers.	übernehmen
arrange	The books in the library are *arranged* according to subjects.	(an-, ein-)ordnen, einrichten
pants/panties		Unterhose, Schlüpfer
sharp		schlau, pfiffig, gewitzt
evergreen ['---]	a tree that stays green even in winter	Immergrün
veteran ['vetərən]	an old car (built before 1916)	Oldtimer
gimmick ['gɪmɪk]		(Werbe-)Gag
compère ['kɒmpeə]		Showmaster
tick-tock ['-'-]	the noise that a clock makes	ticktack
pidgin (English) ['pɪdʒɪn]		Pidgin-Englisch
thoroughly ['θʌrəlɪ]	completely Sid is *thoroughly* fed up with his old car.	völlig, gänzlich, absolut, gründlich
within [wɪð'ɪn]	in, inside Come back soon. Be back *within* a week. Jeremy lives *within* a mile of his school.	in, innerhalb
apart from [ə'pɑːt]	in addition to, except for, not counting Richard owns two cars *apart from* this one. *Apart from* the ending Liz liked the film.	abgesehen von, außer
Welsh	a language spoken in parts of Wales	Walisisch
Gaelic ['geɪlɪk]		Gälisch
the Irish	Irish people, people born in Ireland	die Iren
vowel ['vaʊəl]	"A, e, i, o, u" are all *vowels*.	Vokal, Selbstlaut
vary ['veərɪ]	be/become/make different, change Sometimes it rains, sometimes it snows. The weather *varies* from day to day. Joe's café never *varies* its menu.	(sich) ändern, verändern, unterschiedlich sein
standard	It costs more to send letters that are bigger than the *standard* size. The *standard* language spoken in Germany is called "Hochdeutsch".	Standard-, Norm-, Einheits-
broad [brɔːd]	Arthur speaks with a *broad* Scottish accent. There are a lot of *broad* avenues in Berlin.	stark; breit
region ['riːdʒən]	area, part (of a country)	Gebiet, Gegend
regional ['riːdʒənl]	referring to a particular region	regional, örtlich
shippon ['ʃɪpən]	} cow-house	} Kuhstall
byre ['baɪə]		
beast-house ['biːsthaʊs]		
neat-house ['niːthaʊs]		
cow-stable ['kaʊsteɪbl]		
mistall ['mɪstɔːl]		
western ['westən]		westlich, West-
gravestone ['greɪvstəʊn]	a *gravestone*	Grabstein
RIP ['ɑːraɪ'piː]	short for the Latin expression "requiescat in pace" (let him/her sleep in peace)	Ruhe in Frieden!
taxi ['tæksɪ]	Chris missed the bus, so she took a *taxi*.	Taxi, Taxe
let alone	Liz finds most games complex. She can't follow soccer properly, *let alone* baseball. The Patels haven't got enough money to buy new clothes, *let alone* have a holiday.	geschweige denn, ganz zu schweigen von

Acquisition   **Unit 2**

BBC [biːbiːˈsiː] — Did you know that the *BBC* broadcasts German radio programmes to Germany? — staatl. brit. Rundfunkgesellschaft

newsreader [ˈ---] — somebody who reads the news on the radio or on TV — Nachrichtensprecher(in)

Cockney (adj., n.) [ˈkɒknɪ] — (referring to) an English dialect spoken in London; a person born in a certain part of London — Cockney –; Cockney(dialekt); (echter) Londoner

slang [slæŋ] — colloquial words and phrases, especially those spoken by a particular group
It's often difficult to understand pop fans, crooks, soldiers and schoolchildren, because they use so many *slang* expressions. — nachlässige Umgangssprache; Jargon, der von einzelnen Gruppen gesprochen wird

rhyme (with) [raɪm] — The word "pears" *rhymes with* the word "stairs" and "seen" and "mean" *rhyme*, too. — sich reimen (mit)

If Liz should phone, ... — I don't expect Liz to phone, but if she does, ... — Falls Liz anrufen sollte, ...

distinct [dɪˈstɪŋkt] — easily heard, seen, understood; clear
Good actors can even whisper *distinctly*.
Anne's work shows a *distinct* talent for maths. — deutlich, klar erkennbar

civil service [sɪvlˈsɜːvɪs] — all the government departments except the Army, Navy and Air Force
Civil servants work in the *civil service*. — Staats-, Verwaltungsdienst

advisable [ədˈvaɪzəbl] — Ellen advised Carl to hurry. "It's *advisable* to avoid the rush-hour," she said. — ratsam

acquire [əˈkwaɪə] — The firm has *acquired* a good reputation. — erwerben, (er-)lernen

neutral [ˈnjuːtrəl] — the same as in German — neutral

slight(ly) [slaɪt] — Colin made a *slight* mistake. This was due to the fact that he was *slightly* tired and had a *slight* headache.
Do you like jazz? – Not in the *slightest*. — gering(fügig), etwas, leicht

tolerable [ˈtɒlərəbl] — good enough
The food at Joe's café isn't very good, but it's usually *tolerable*. — erträglich, leidlich

impression [ɪmˈpreʃn] — Barbara was impressed with the car. It made a good *impression* on her. — Eindruck

obstacle [ˈɒbstəkl] — something in the way that stops progress or makes progress difficult — Hindernis

in this/every/no/ some, etc. **respect(s)** — The minister liked the plan *in some respects*, but she didn't like it *in every respect*. — in dieser/jeder/ keiner/mancher usw. Hinsicht

bilingual [baɪˈlɪŋgwəl] — Jeremy speaks two languages like a native. He's *bilingual*. — zweisprachig

2 *T 1   *Some names referring to people or languages:*

Swedish [ˈswiːdɪʃ] — Schwedisch — Saxon (adj., n.) [ˈsæksən] — sächsisch; Sachse, Sächsin
Danish [ˈdeɪnɪʃ] — Dänisch — Anglo-Saxon [ˈæŋgləʊˈsæksən] — Angelsächsisch
Dane [deɪn] — Däne, Dänin — Germanic [dʒɜːˈmænɪk] — Germanisch
Celt [kelt] — Kelte, Keltin — Viking [ˈvaɪkɪŋ] — Wikinger(in)
Celtic (adj., n.) [ˈkeltɪk] — keltisch; Keltisch — Norwegian [nɔːˈwiːdʒən] — Norweger(in)
Roman [ˈrəʊmən] — Römer(in) — Norman (adj., n.) [ˈnɔːmən] — normannisch; Normanne, Normannin
the Angles [ˈæŋglz] — die Angeln
the Jutes [dʒuːts] — die Jüten

131

Unit 2

*Text 1

BC [ˈbiːˈsiː]		short for "before (the birth of) Christ"	v. Chr.
AD [ˈeɪˈdiː]		short for the Latin expression "anno Domini" meaning "after the birth of Christ"	n. Chr.
survive [səˈvaɪv]		Only one of the passengers didn't die in the crash. She was lucky. She *survived*.	überleben
invade [ɪnˈveɪd]		In 1939 Germany *invaded* Poland.	einmarschieren, einfallen in
Christianization [krɪstjənaɪˈzeɪʃn]			Bekehrung zum Christentum, Christianisierung
conquest [ˈkɒŋkwest] conqueror [ˈkɒŋkərə]		William's army won England by force. This *conquest* made him the most famous *conqueror* in the history of England.	Eroberung Eroberer
poetry [ˈpəʊɪtrɪ]		Heinrich Heine wrote a lot of poems. His *poetry* is often sad.	Poesie, poetische Dichtung, Gedicht
reinforce [riːɪnˈfɔːs]		make stronger (by adding something) Mrs Carey's front door is *reinforced* with iron bars.	verstärken, untermauern, kräftigen
printing press [ˈprɪntɪŋpres]		an old-fashioned *printing press*	Druckerpresse, Druckmaschine
c. [ˈsɜːkə]		short form for "about, roughly"	ca.
sky [skaɪ]		There are two clouds in the *sky*.	Himmel
prince [prɪns]		the title of the son of a king or queen	Prinz
baron [ˈbærən]		This title is used in German, too.	Baron
1 calf, 2 calves [kɑːf, kɑːvz]		a cow with two *calves*	ein Kalb, zwei Kälber
veal [viːl]		meat from a calf	Kalbfleisch
mutton [ˈmʌtn]		meat from a sheep	Hammelfleisch
uisge [ˈwɪsgɪ]		the Celts' word for "water", used in their expression for "whisky" (water of life)	Whisky
2 T 2	**pick up**	learn without taking lessons or studying Bill *picked up* a little Italian during his holiday.	mitbekommen, „aufschnappen"
	tolerable [ˈtɒlərəbl]	good enough	erträglich, leidlich
	working knowledge	necessary, basic knowledge Mr Lee can order a meal in French or ask the way, but not discuss literature. He's got a *working knowledge* of French.	ausreichende (Grund-)Kenntnisse
	perfect [ˈpɜːfɪkt]	complete, excellent, with no faults It's *perfectly* clear that Cathy and John understand each other *perfectly*. She's a *perfect* wife and he's a *perfect* husband.	vollkommen, vollendet, perfekt
	consolation [kɒnsəˈleɪʃn]	Colin tried to cheer Jean up, because she was sad and needed some *consolation*.	Trost, Tröstung
	yet (adv.)	The table was already full. But the film star invited *yet* more guests to join her.	(sogar) noch
	amazement [əˈmeɪzmənt]	great surprise Ray was amazed. He looked at the girl in *amazement*. To his *amazement* he knew her.	Erstaunen
	posses [pəˈzes]	own, have The immigrants *possessed* only a few clothes.	besitzen, haben

Text 2

Unit 2

light,	After *lighting* the candles on the Christmas tree,	(sich) anzünden
I lit,	Christine *lit* a cigarette.	
I've lit	The boys *lit* the fire too near their tent.	
mutter ['mʌtə]	The pupils at the back of the class always *mutter* when the new teacher is teaching.	murmeln
be/get accustomed to [ə'kʌstəmd]	be/get used to Mr and Mrs Day *are accustomed to* going to church on Sundays. They *got accustomed to* this when they were children.	gewöhnt sein an, es gewohnt sein, sich gewöhnen an
a **most** important lady	an extremely important lady Fiona met a *most* exciting writer recently.	eine äußerst wichtige Dame
soft	the opposite of "hard"; quiet Lisa has got a *soft* voice, but she doesn't always speak *softly*. Sometimes she shouts. Tom hates hard beds. He prefers *soft* ones.	sanft, weich, leise
abominable [ə'bɒmɪnəbl]	terrible, extremely unpleasant The service in Joe's café is *abominable*. All wars are *abominable*.	scheußlich, schrecklich, abscheulich
anyway	in any case, whatever else might happen	jedenfalls
business	affair, subject, thing Doing homework is often a boring *business*.	Sache, Angelegenheit
the other day/week	a few days/weeks ago Have you heard from Rosemary recently? – Yes, she phoned me just *the other week*.	neulich, vor ein paar Tagen/ Wochen
alien (n.) ['eɪljən]	a foreign citizen; s.b. from another planet Customs officers often check the luggage of *aliens* particularly carefully.	Ausländer(in), Fremde(r), Fremdling
alien (adj.)	strange, foreign; from another planet	fremd; fremdartig

2 T 3

limerick ['lɪmərɪk]	a funny poem that consists of five lines	(5zeiliger Unsinnvers)
verse [vɜːs]	Poems are written in *verse* (form). Do you know the second *verse* of the song?	Vers, Versform; Poesie; Strophe
rhyme (n.)	"Hat" rhymes with "cat". "Flat" is a *rhyme* as well.	Reim, Reimwort

2 Ex

invest [ɪn'vest]	Tom has *invested* £100 in his sister's boutique.	investieren, anlegen
proverb ['prɒvɜːb]	"If two men ride on a horse, one must ride behind." is a *proverb* about leaders.	Sprichwort, Spruch
hitch-hike ['hɪtʃhaɪk]	make a journey by hitching lifts Alfred and Eva *hitch-hiked* to Hull last year.	per Anhalter fahren, trampen
prepositional phrase [prepə'zɪʃənl]	"Due to" is an example of a *prepositional phrase*.	präpositionale Wendung
hesitate ['hezɪteɪt]	make a short pause, especially when unsure	zögern
gap [gæp]	an unfilled space Jerry waited for a *gap* in the traffic before crossing the road.	Lücke, Spalte, Öffnung, Zwischenraum, -zeit
bridge a gap	Herb and Louise got to the station early. So, to *bridge the gap* until their train arrived, they had a cup of tea.	eine Lücke ausfüllen, die Zwischenzeit überbrücken
lengthen ['leŋθən]	Lisa's old skirts were too short for the new fashion, so she *lengthened* them. In Europe the days *lengthen* in March.	(sich) verlängern, ausdehnen, länger werden

Unit 2

Exercises

as a matter of fact	to be honest, in fact, really, actually Ian isn't really ill, you know. *As a matter of fact,* I saw him at the disco last night.	um ehrlich zu sein, in der Tat
The thing is, ...	Liz wants a car but, *the thing is,* she can't really afford the insurance, etc.	Die Sache ist nämlich die, ...
... as I say ...	I dislike jazz, *as I say,* I prefer pop.	..., wie ich sagte, ...
There's something in it.	The PM thinks *there's something in* the story.	Da ist etwas dran.

2 S **transitive** ['trænsɪtɪv] A *transitive* verb is one that's used with a direct object. In "Al used to smoke 20 cigarettes a day.", the verb "smoke" is used *transitively*. transitiv

intransitive The verb "smoke" is used without a direct object in "Al doesn't smoke now.". It's *intransitive* here. intransitiv

inversion [ɪn'vɜːʃn] changing the order of words in a sentence, e.g. turning the form "I can" into "Can I?" Inversion

in now way in keinem Fall

omission [ə'mɪʃn] leaving out, being left out
The boss spotted an *omission* in the list. Aus-, Weg-, Unterlassung

Unit 3

3 A **lightning** ['laɪtnɪŋ] light caused by electricity during a storm
That old tree was struck by *lightning*. Blitz(e)

a flash of lightning Liz and Jeremy were playing golf, when suddenly there was a *flash of lightning*. ein Blitz

ghetto ['getəʊ] a poor part of a town, lived in by people who are discriminated against, e.g. because of their race or religion Getto; von einer (ethnischen) Minderheit bewohntes Elendsviertel

loot [luːt] steal from, rob (aus-)plündern

blackout ['--] A *blackout* can be caused by too many people using electricity at the same time. totaler Stromausfall

be shocked at Lynn was *shocked at* the news. erschüttert, entrüstet sein über

snowstorm ['--] similar to the German word Schneesturm

° = degree [dɪ'griː] The usual temperature of your blood is about 37°C (37 *degrees centigrade*). Grad

C = centigrade ['sentɪgreɪd] Water freezes at about 0°C. Celsius

heat make warm or hot (be-)heizen

heating Bill's central *heating* has got nine radiators. Heizung

freeze to death die through being cold erfrieren

crisis, crises ['kraɪsɪs, 'kraɪsiːz] time(s) of trouble, danger or problems Krise, -n

Arab (adj., n.) ['ærəb] referring to Egypt, Saudi Arabia, Jordan, etc; somebody from one of these countries arabisch; Araber(in)

Israeli (adj., n.) [ɪz'reɪlɪ] referring to Israel; a citizen of Israel israelisch; Israeli

supply, supplies [sə'plaɪ, sə'plaɪz] The astronauts took a large *supply* of technical equipment with them, as well as food *supplies* and medicine. Vorrat, -räte; Bestand; Versorgung, Nachschub

scarce [skeəs] knapp

embargo [em'bɑːgəʊ] The same word is used in German. Embargo, Handelssperre, Lieferstopp

Acquisition

Unit 3

increase (in) (n.) ['--]	an extra amount (of), more The *increase in* crime worried the mayor.	Erhöhung, Anstieg
increase (v.) [-'-]	become or make bigger, higher The police car *increased* its speed. The population of India *increased* last year.	erhöhen, zunehmen, (sich) vergrößern
barrel ['bærəl]	a unit of measurement for oil (159 litres)	Barrel
import (into ... from) (v.) [ɪm'pɔːt]	bring into a country Wine is *imported into* Germany *from* France.	importieren, einführen (nach/in ... aus)
import (n.) ['--]	French wine is one of Germany's *imports*.	Import; Einfuhr
become/be aware (of) [ə'weə]	Ben *became aware of* the danger he was in. The mayor *wasn't aware of* the new plans. He *wasn't aware* that they'd been changed.	(be-)merken; wissen (von); sich (einer Sache) bewußt werden/sein
be unaware (of s.th.)	Tony *was unaware of* the danger. He *was unaware* that he was in danger.	sich (einer Sache) nicht bewußt sein
dependence (on) [dɪ'pendəns]	being dependent (on), opposite of "independence (from)"	Abhängigkeit (von)
gas, gases [gæs, 'gæsɪz]	Air is a mixture of different *gases*.	Gas, Gase
natural gas ['nætʃrəl'gæs]	We use *natural gas* for cooking and heating.	Erdgas
energy ['enədʒɪ]	similar to the German word	Energie
form	Will Labour *form* the next government? Dark clouds *formed* in the north.	(sich) bilden, gestalten
car pool ['--]	Mr Lee gives his neighbour a lift to work on Mondays, his neighbour gives him a lift on Tuesdays, etc. They run a *car pool*.	Fahrgemeinschaft
measure ['meʒə]	The army took *measures* to stop the looting.	Maßnahme
back to normal	normal again	wieder normal
diagram ['daɪəgræm]	similar to the German word	Diagram
consumption [kən'sʌmʃn]	A lot of beer is consumed in Germany. The *consumption* of beer is quite high here.	Verbrauch, Konsum
rise [raɪz], **it rose** [rəʊz], **it's risen** ['rɪzn]	Prices keep going up. Prices keep *rising*. The sun made the temperature *rise*.	(an-, auf-) steigen
fossil fuels ['fɒslfjʊəlz]	coal, natural gas and oil	fossile Brennstoffe
exhaustible [ɪg'zɔːstəbl]	Libya's reserves of oil are *exhaustible*. Tom's boss never gets exhausted. Her strength seems to be *inexhaustible*.	erschöpfbar
inexhaustible		unerschöpflich
run out (of)	The ship's food supplies *ran out*. The crew *ran out of* food.	ausgehen, zu Ende gehen
below (prep., adv.) [bɪ'ləʊ]	Val's test result was *below* average. The people in the flat *below* are friendly.	unter(halb); unten
surface ['sɜːfɪs]	Rosemary's head is above the *surface*. Her body is below it.	Oberfläche
(coal-, gas-, oil-)field	There's a big *coal-field* near Bolsover. There are *oil-fields* under the North Sea.	(Kohle-)Revier, (Gas-, Öl-)Feld
deposit [dɪ'pɒzɪt]	The company discovered a new *deposit* of coal.	Vorkommen, Lager(stätte)
alternative (adj.)	Bad weather over Frankfurt forced the plane to land at an *alternative* airport.	anderer, (-e, -es), Ersatz-, Ausweich-
accurate ['ækjʊrət]	exact	genau, exakt
adviser (on) [əd'vaɪzə]	somebody who gives advice (on)	Berater (für, in)
crude oil ['kruːdɔɪl]	oil as it is found in nature	Rohöl

Unit 3

Acquisition

refine [rɪ'faɪn]	make purer or cleaner Sugar is *refined* before we eat it.	raffinieren
fuel oil ['--]	oil used for heating, engines, etc.	Heiz-, Treiböl
plastic	Cheap toys are often made of *plastic*.	Kunststoff
manufacture [mænjʊ'fæktʃə]	make (usually in a factory) British Leyland *manufacture* vehicles.	herstellen, erzeugen
coke [kəʊk]	Mrs Bell put some more *coke* on the fire.	Koks
drive (a machine)	make (a machine) work That old engine is *driven* by coal.	(eine Maschine) antreiben
turbine ['tɜːbaɪn]	the same as in German	Turbine
generate ['dʒenəreɪt]	produce The experiment *generated* a violent reaction.	erzeugen, bilden, hervorrufen
uranium [jʊ'reɪnjəm]	a raw material used to produce nuclear power	Uran
nuclear fission ['fɪʃn]		Kernspaltung
convert (into) [kən'vɜːt]	Sunshine can be *converted into* electricity. The old church was *converted into* a cinema.	umwandeln (in), umformen (zu)
nuclear fusion ['fjuːzn]		Kernverschmelzung
total	total number or amount Liz spent a *total* of £25 altogether.	Summe, Gesamt- menge, Gesamtheit
industrial [ɪn'dʌstrɪəl]	Office workers sometimes don't understand the problems faced by *industrial* workers.	industriell, Industrie- Fabrik-
household ['--]	similar to the German word	(Privat-)Haushalt
growth [grəʊθ]	(the result of) growing Population *growth* causes problems in cities. The baby grew fast. Its *growth* was amazing.	Wachstum, Zunahme, Zuwachs
per capita consumption [pə'kæpɪtə]	consumption per person	Pro-Kopf- Verbrauch
developing country	a nation with a low economic level	Entwicklungsland
industrialized country [ɪn'dʌstrɪəlaɪzd]	a country with well-developed industries based on modern technology	Industrieland, -staat, -nation
kilogram of coal equivalent	a unit of measurement for comparing different sources of energy	Steinkohlen- einheit (SKE)
constant ['kɒnstənt]	staying the same, not changing, steady A sudden fire is a *constant* risk in discos.	ständig, stetig, konstant
non-renewable [--'---]	that can run out but can't be replaced, exhaustible	nicht erneuerbar
search for (v.)	look for The police *searched for* the lost children and used dogs in the *search (for)* them, too.	suchen (nach)
search (for) (n.)		Suche (nach)
drill (v.)	use a machine to make a hole	bohren
drill (n.)	a machine for making holes	Bohrer
drilling		Bohrung
oil rig ['--]		Bohrinsel
profitable ['----]	*Profitable* firms make a profit. Reading good literature is very *profitable*.	lohnend, einträglich, gewinnbringend
find	something that's discovered	Fund
exploit [ɪk'splɔɪt]	The oil under the North Sea is being *exploited* now.	fördern, erschließen; ausbeuten
transport [-'-]	An oil-tanker *transports* oil.	transportieren
environment [ɪn'vaɪərənmənt]	Factories shouldn't pollute the *environment*. A child's development is influenced by his or her home *environment*. Eve's school is in a rural *environment*.	Umwelt, Umgebung
factor ['fæktə]	similar to the German word	Faktor
pipeline ['--]	We use the same word in German.	Ölleitung, Pipeline

Acquisition

Unit 3

prevent (from ... ing) [prɪ'vent]	stop (from ... ing) Liz *prevented* a possible crash. She *prevented* her drunken friend *from* driv*ing* his car.	verhüten, vorbeugen, hindern (an), abhalten (von)
economical [i:kə'nɒmɪkl]	not causing waste or unnecessary costs Is it *economical* to transport coal by air?	sparsam, wirtschaftlich, kostensparend
urgent ['ɜ:dʒənt]	The voice on the phone spoke *urgently:* "Will you hurry, doctor? It's *urgent*. Please!"	(ein-)dringlich, dringend
involve (in) [ɪn'vɒlv]	have as a necessary consequence The risks *involved in* the plan are too big. Nick's new job will *involve* living abroad.	verbunden sein mit, mit sich bringen, verknüpfen mit
tides [taɪdz]		Gezeiten
tidal ['taɪdl]		Gezeiten-
radioactive [---'--]	similar to the German word	radioaktiv
a room of my own	Abdul shares his kitchen with a neighbour. But Juanita has got a kitchen *of her own*.	ein eigenes Zimmer, ein Zimmer für mich
waste	rubbish	Müll, Abfall
waste-disposal [dɪ'spəʊzl]	getting rid of waste	Müllbeseitigung, Entsorgung
safety	being safe	Sicherheit
solar ['səʊlə]	referring to the sun	Sonnen-, Solar-
install [ɪn'stɔ:l]	Frank had the know-how to *install* his new central heating system himself.	einbauen, -richten, montieren
store	keep for later Don't *store* ice-cream in a warm place!	speichern, einlagern, (auf-)bewahren
unpredictable [--'---]	something that cannot be predicted	nicht voraussagbar
technological progress [teknə'lɒdʒɪkl]	progress in the field of technology	technologischer Fortschritt
conservation [kɒnsə'veɪʃn]	avoiding waste, saving energy, protecting historic buildings, the environment, etc. To protect their local countryside, Jean and Colin formed a nature *conservation* society.	Erhaltung, Bewahrung, Schutz
conserve [kən'sɜ:v]	If we want to have a supply of wood in future, we must *conserve* our forests.	sparsam umgehen mit, erhalten
(in-)efficient [ɪ'fɪʃənt]	(not) able to work well, with little waste of energy, time, material, etc. Old-fashioned machines are often *inefficient*.	(nicht) sparsam, wirksam, rationell
insulation [ɪnsjʊ'leɪʃn]	Drawn curtains can act as *insulation*, helping to keep a house or flat warm.	Isolierung
recycle [ri:'saɪkl]	make use of something again and again	wiederverwerten
aluminium [ælə'mɪnjəm]	the same as in German	Aluminium
do ... miles per gallon	consume 1 gallon of petrol per ... miles	... l/100 km verbrauchen
concerned (about) [kən'sɜ:nd]	worried (about)	besorgt (um)
nor [nɔ:]	"and not" after a negative statement	und/auch ... nicht
pursue [pə'sju:]	The government is *pursuing* a new policy. A helpful stranger *pursued* the pickpocket.	verfolgen
believe in	Peter *believes in* life after death. Anne *believes in* getting a lot of exercise.	glauben an; viel halten von
3 T **take** time **off**	Janet had to go to the doctor's, so she *took* the morning *off* (work/school).	sich (Zeit) freinehmen
cheerful ['--]	Cheer up, Herb. Try to be *cheerful* again.	heiter, fröhlich

Unit 3   Text

leaf, leaves [li:f, li:vz]	two leaves	Blatt, Blätter
pale [peɪl]	Jerry's face went white. He turned *pale*.	blaß, bleich
tense	affected by stress and a nervous feeling. The robber's face was hard and *tense*.	(an-)gespannt, verkrampft
love		Liebling, Schatz
boot [bu:t]	the *boot*	Kofferraum
alcohol [ˈælkəhɒl]	similar to the German word	Alkohol
paperback (adj., n.)	Monica never buys expensive books, she only buys *paperback* editions / *paperbacks*.	Taschenbuch(-)
novel [ˈnɒvl]	a long story, e.g. 'Der Butt'	Roman
transfer [trænsˈfɜ:]	Mr Bell no longer works in this bank. He's been *transferred* to a different branch. Al *transferred* his skills to the new problem.	versetzen, -legen; übertragen
graduate [ˈgrædʒʊət]	Christine has just passed her final exams at university. She's a *graduate* now.	Hochschulabsolvent(in)
engineer [endʒɪˈnɪə]	similar to the German word	Ingenieur(in)
engineering [endʒɪˈnɪərɪŋ]	the technology of building or designing machines, bridges, tunnels, cars, etc.	Ingenieurwesen, Technik
bright	John had to put his sun-glasses on, because the sunshine was too *bright* for his eyes.	hell, glänzend, leuchtend
platform	similar to the German word	Plattform
shift	Fred's night-*shift* lasts from 10 pm to 6 am.	(Arbeits-)Schicht
antiseptic [--ˈ--]	similar to the German word	antiseptisch, keimtötend
smell	Can you smell anything? – Yes, it's the *smell* of fried onions coming from the kitchen.	Geruch, Duft, Gestank
sour [ˈsaʊə]	opposite of "sweet"	sauer
mud [mʌd]	When Miss Davies came in from the garden, there was a lot of *mud* on her shoes.	Bohrschlamm, Spülflüssigkeit
mudman, mud engineer	an oil rig worker specializing in the mud that's used in drilling	Bohrschlamm-Spezialist
mud room	the room in which a mud engineer does tests and mixes the mud used in drilling	Spülungsraum
mud pit	a big tank in which drilling mud is mixed	Spülungsmischbehälter
sleeping-quarters		Schlafquartier
silence [ˈsaɪləns]	"Be quiet!" the teacher shouted. *"Silence!"* No-one spoke. The *silence* lasted for 5 minutes.	Ruhe, Stille, Schweigen
pump [pʌmp]	Some factories *pump* waste into rivers.	pumpen
bit	the part of a drill that actually cuts	(Bohr-)Meißel, Bohrspitze
blow-out	an accident in which a large amount of oil or gas suddenly escapes from a hole during drilling	(unkontrollierter) Öl- bzw. Gas-
fear [fɪə]	be frightened of, be afraid of. Liz *fears* lightning more than anything else.	(be-)fürchten, Angst haben vor
Norwegian [nɔːˈwiːdʒən]	referring to Norway	norwegisch
unimaginable	something that cannot be imagined	unvorstellbar
roustabout [ˈraʊstəbaʊt]	an unskilled worker on an oil rig	Hilfsarbeiter
sample [ˈsɑːmpl]	part of s.th. taken to show what the rest is like. Sue examined *samples* of different carpets.	Probe, Muster
well-hole [ˈ--]		Bohrloch
midnight [ˈ--]	12 o'clock at night	Mitternacht

Unit 3

Text

helmet [′helmɪt]	two *helmets*	Helm
weathered [′weðəd]	affected by the sun, wind, etc.	vom Wetter gegerbt, verwittert
tool pusher [′---]	the top man on an oil rig, "the captain"	Bohrmeister
envy s.b. (s.th.) [′envɪ]	Freddie would love to have Russel's super job. Freddie *envies* Russell (his job).	jn. (um etwas) beneiden
by the way	an expression used to introduce a new topic of conversation Oh, *by the way,* are you busy tonight, Carl?	nebenbei (bemerkt), übrigens
yawn [jɔ:n]	Ellen was tired and bored. She's couldn't stop *yawning.*	gähnen
bunk [bʌŋk]	the top *bunk* / the bottom *bunk*	Koje, Etagenbett
off duty	not working, not on duty	dienstfrei
remind s.b. of/to do s.th. [rɪ′maɪnd]	The photo made Dave remember his holiday in Munich. It *reminded* him *of* his stay there. Jeremy *reminded* Anne *to* buy the tickets.	jn. an etwas erinnern/daran erinnern, etwas zu tun
lonely [′ləʊnlɪ]	(sad from) being on your own, without company	einsam, verlassen
loneliness [′---]	state of feeling lonely	Einsamkeit
leave	a holiday for people in the army, for workers on a contract away from home, etc. Herb is home on *leave* from his job in Brazil.	Urlaub
lifeblood [′--]	s.th. that gives strength and energy	Herzblut
hero [′hɪərəʊ]	a man or boy who's earned respect for brave actions; the main character in a novel, film, etc.	Held; Hauptperson
heroine [′herəʊɪn]	a female hero	Heldin
geologist [dʒɪ′ɒlədʒɪst]	a scientist who has studied the earth's history and is an expert on rocks, etc.	Geologe, Geologin
incident [′ɪnsɪdənt]	A small *incident* changed Brian's life.	Zwischenfall, Vorfall, Episode
preventer [prɪ′ventə]		Preventer (Absperrvorrichtung zur Vermeidung eines unkontrollierten Öl- bzw. Gasausbruchs)
deck	the same as in German	Deck
(hard)-featured [′hɑ:d′fi:tʃəd]	The crook had a cold, hard-*featured* face. Al is soft-*featured,* but a hard businessman.	mit (harten, groben) Gesichtszügen
roughneck [′rʌfnek]	a skilled worker on oil rigs	Bohrfacharbeiter
wop	racialist slang for somebody from Italy	"Itaker"
fist	two pairs of *fists*	Faust
dawn [dɔ:n]	the time when the sun starts to rise The submarine entered the harbour at *dawn.*	Morgengrauen, -dämmerung
panic [′pænɪk]	similar to the German word	Panik
sky [skaɪ], sometimes **skies**	There are clouds in the *sky.* It's going to rain, I bet.	Himmel
noon [nu:n]	12 o'clock in the morning, mid-day	Mittag
prisoner [′prɪznə]	somebody who's in prison or not free The king's daughter was taken *prisoner* and held *prisoner* for 2 years.	Gefangene(r)

Unit 3

Exercises

3 Ex	**Zambian** (adj., n.) [ˈzæmbɪən]	referring to Zambia; a native of Zambia	sambisch; Sambier(in)
	copy	The sales manager asked his secretary to photocopy the letter. He wanted 3 *copies*. Have you seen a *copy* of today's paper?	Kopie; Exemplar
	anorak [ˈænəræk]	the same as in German	Anorak
	path [pɑːθ]	a place for people to walk, not for vehicles Don't go on the road. Keep on the *path*.	Pfad, Weg
	style [staɪl]	Experts can usually judge who painted a picture by studying the *style* it's painted in. Liz hates Mr Maxwell's *style* of teaching.	Stil, Art, Weise
	put right	The new boss tried to solve the firm's problems. He tried to *put* everything *right*.	in Ordnung bringen
	put up (prices)	make (prices) higher, make (prices) go up	(Preise) erhöhen
	respond (to) [rɪˈspɒnd]	react (to), reply (to)	reagieren (auf), antworten (auf)
	I'd rather you stayed.	I'd prefer it if you stayed. Pat *would rather* you didn't invite Shaun to the party. She*'d rather* not see him.	Mir wäre es lieber, wenn du bliebest.
	a lot to ask (of s.b.)	Ellen asked Carl to lay the table. That wasn't *a lot to ask* (*of* him), was it?	viel verlangt (von jm.)
	You're welcome to.	May I borrow your tennis racket, Jenny? – Sure. *You're welcome to.*	Gerne./Aber natürlich./Bitte schön.
	move up	Everyone in the queue *moved up* one place. If we *move up,* Tom can sit on the sofa, too.	vor-, weiter-, aufrücken
3 S	**intention** [ɪnˈtenʃn]	What do you intend to do, Lisa? What are your *intentions*?	Absicht, Vorhaben
	deduction [dɪˈdʌkʃn]	If only birds can fly and budgies can fly, it's a safe *deduction* that budgies are birds.	Schlußfolgerung

Unit 4

4 A/T	**contain** [kənˈteɪn]	What's the book's content? What does it *contain*?	enthalten
	narrative text [ˈnærətɪv]		erzählender Text
	critical [ˈkrɪtɪkl]	The coach criticized Tommy. He made *critical* remarks about how Tommy had played.	kritisch
	thoroughly [ˈθʌrəlɪ]	The police searched the van *thoroughly.*	sorgfältig, genau, gründlich
	section [ˈsekʃn]	a separate part The first *section* of the motorway is finished.	Teil, Abschnitt
	work of art, music, etc.	Have you read any of G.B. Shaw's *works*? The pianist played a *work* by Brahms.	(Kunst-)Werk
	fiction [ˈfɪkʃn]	Real life can be stranger than *fiction*. Have you read any good *fiction* lately?	Dichtung, erzählende Literatur
	work of fiction	Kafka's "Schloß" is a *work of fiction*.	Prosawerk, -text
	aid [eɪd]	help Language labs are an *aid* to learning English. Have you got a first *aid* box in your car? The king asked for emergency *aid* from abroad.	Hilfe, Hilfsmittel
	appreciation [əpriːʃɪˈeɪʃn]		kritische Würdigung Interpretation, Analyse

140

Acquisition / Text

Unit 4

summarize [ˈsʌməraɪz]	make a summary of Liz *summarized* the story in a few sentences.	zusammenfassen
author [ˈɔːθə]	another word for "writer", "lady writer"	Schriftsteller(in), Dichter(in)
poetry [ˈpəʊɪtrɪ]	Heinrich Heine wrote a lot of poems. His *poetry* is often sad.	Poesie, poetische Dichtung, Gedichte
stanza [ˈstænzə]	The poem on page 81 has got 3 *stanzas*.	Strophe
scheme [skiːm]	pattern, system, arrangement Two pupils didn't plan their work properly. There was no *scheme* in what they wrote.	Schema, System
metre		Versmaß, Metrum
foot		(Vers-)Fuß
rhythm [ˈrɪðəm]	similar to the German word	Rhythmus
correspond (to/with) [kɒrɪˈspɒnd]	Albert tells lies. His words don't *correspond with* the truth. A-levels *correspond to* the "Abitur".	in Einklang stehen (mit), passen (zu), entsprechen
poet [ˈpəʊɪt]	somebody who writes poetry	Dichter(in), Lyriker(in)
subject matter [ˈ----]	topic of a conversation, discussion, story, report, etc.	Gegenstand, Inhalt, Stoff
theme [θiːm]	similar to the German word	Thema
setting	where a story takes place, e.g. in "Robinson Crusoe" it's an island	Schauplatz
atmosphere [ˈætməsfɪə]	similar to the German word The *atmosphere* in Joe's café is friendly.	Atmosphäre
create [kriːˈeɪt]	make, produce, generate, give birth to Jeff's behaviour *created* a bad impression. Nobody knows when the earth was *created*.	erzeugen, (er-)schaffen
tone	Mr Rose is a popular teacher. The pupils like his informal *tone*.	Ton, Haltung
playful	full of fun, not serious, not meant seriously	spielerisch, munter, heiter
ironic(al) [aɪˈrɒnɪkl]	It was pouring with rain. "It's a lovely day today, isn't it?" Wag said *ironically*.	ironisch
irony [ˈaɪərənɪ]	a technique of expressing ideas more effectively, either by saying something indirectly or by saying the opposite of what's meant	Ironie
image [ˈɪmɪdʒ]	a picture painted with words	(Wort-)Bild, bildlicher Ausdruck
simile [ˈsɪmɪlɪ]	"He's as brave as a lion." is an example of a *simile*.	Vergleich, Gleichnis
metaphor [ˈmetəfə]	"Jill flew out of the room." is an example of a *metaphor* – unless Jill was a budgie!	Metapher
additional [əˈdɪʃənl]	extra, further, in addition	zusätzlich
connotation [kɒnəˈteɪʃn]	an extra meaning that a word can have for a person, apart from its basic meaning Sue lives near an airport. When she hears the word "plane", she thinks of "noise". For her the *connotation* of "plane" is "noise".	Nebenbedeutung, Beiklang
analyse [ˈænəlaɪz]	similar to the German word	analysieren, genau untersuchen
symbolic [sɪmˈbɒlɪk]	Some flowers are a symbol of love. Flowers can have other *symbolic* meanings, too.	symbolisch, sinnbildlich
interpret [-ˈ--]	make clear, decide what something means It was hard to *interpret* Lisa's behaviour.	interpretieren, auslegen, deuten

Unit 4
Acquisition/Text

interpretation [ɪntɜːprɪˈteɪʃn]	Ed didn't interpret the ending like Sue. His *interpretation* of it was different.	Auslegung, Deutu Interpretation
beauty [ˈbjuːtɪ]	Liz was beautiful and Al loved her *beauty*.	Schönheit
dot	There are 3 *dots* at the end of this line ...	Punkt, Pünktchen
print [prɪnt]	Newspapers, books, etc. are *printed*.	drucken
function [ˈfʌŋkʃn]	What's the heart for? – It pumps blood around the body. That's its *function*.	Funktion
division [dɪˈvɪʒn]	(the result of) being divided, dividing	Trennung, (Auf-)Teilung
parody [ˈpærədɪ]	similar to the German word	Parodie
amuse [əˈmjuːz]	Mike told jokes and *amused* everybody. While their parents talked about politics, the children *amused* themselves in the garden.	amüsieren, unterhalten, zum Lach bringen
imitate [ˈɪmɪteɪt]	The monkeys copied the way Rex moved. They *imitated* his movements.	imitieren, nachahmen, -machen
fairy-story [ˈfeərɪstɔːrɪ]	Can you remember any of the *fairy-stories* by the Brothers Grimm?	Märchen
Little Red Riding Hood [hʊd] [---ˈ---]		Rotkäppchen
comic	*Comic* material is written by *comic* writers in order to make people laugh.	komisch, lustig, humoristisch
fable [ˈfeɪbl]	a kind of fairy-story in which the actions of animals can teach you something	(Tier-)Fabel
element [ˈelɪmənt]	The same word is used in German.	Element, Bestand
accusation [ækjʊˈzeɪʃn]	The police accused Tom of robbing the bank, but the *accusation* wasn't justified.	An-, Beschuldigur Anklage, Vorwur
banish [ˈbænɪʃ]	send away (out of the country)	verbannen, ausweisen
satire [ˈsætaɪə]		Satire, Spottgedicht, -schrift
still	in spite of this Al felt sick, but he *still* went to the party.	dennoch, trotzdem
short story [ˈ-ˈ--]	E.A. Poe wrote a lot of *short stories*.	Kurzgeschichte, Erzählung
exposition [ekspəˈzɪʃn]	a part of a film, novel, etc., usually at the beginning, which says what the film, etc. is about	Exposition, Einführung
move on	continue, develop	weitergehen, fortschreiten
suspense [səˈspens]	The film made Lisa excited. How would it end? She could hardly stand the *suspense*.	Spannung
build up to	Kathy and Ray kept criticizing each other. It soon *built up to* a violent argument.	sich entwickeln zu gipfeln in
climax [ˈklaɪmæks]	the most interesting or exciting point of a story, adventure, sports event, etc.	Krise, Höhepunkt, Gipfel
solution [səˈluːʃn]	Ellen finally solved the problem, but it wasn't easy to find the *solution*.	(Auf-)Lösung, Erklärung
open-ended [ˈ--ˈ--]	without a clear ending; without a time limit Did Pete take the job at ECA? – Well, no-one knows for sure. The story is *open-ended*. The meeting is *open-ended*. Nobody knows when it will end.	offen, mit ungewissem Ausgan
flashback [ˈ--]	part of a story that goes back in time to show what happened earlier in the story	Rückblende, -blick
limit (to)	Speed limits tell you to *limit* your speed. Sandra invited 5 people to her party. She *limited* the invitations *to* her best friends.	begrenzen, beschränken (auf

142

Acquisition / Text

Unit 4

characterize ['kærəktəraɪz] characterization [kærəktəraɪ'zeɪʃn]	describe the character of Liz *characterized* Mr Maxwell as a lazy idiot, but none of the other pupils agreed with this unkind *characterization*.	beschreiben, charakterisieren Beschreibung, Charakterisierung
explicit [ɪk'splɪsɪt]	expressed directly	ausdrücklich, direkt
implicit [ɪm'plɪsɪt]	expressed indirectly "Stop telling such silly jokes." is an *explicit* remark. "I've heard you tell better jokes." is an *implicit* remark.	(mit) einbegriffen, indirekt
contribute (to) [kən'trɪbjuːt]	make a contribution (to) Lisa *contributed* a lot (*to* the success).	beitragen, beisteuern (zu)
science fiction [--'--]	fiction which shows how future developments in science could affect people's lives	Zukunftsroman(e), „Science-fiction"
parallel ['pærəlel]	A-level exams and the "Abitur" are similar. There are lots of *parallels* between them.	Parallele, Ähnlichkeit, Entsprechung

Ex

chat	a friendly informal conversation	Schwatz, Geplauder, Unterhaltung
festival ['festɪvəl]	Steve Studd's latest film was given a prize at the Berlin Film *Festival*. Tom's church is holding a *festival* at Easter.	Festwoche(n), Festspiele, Festspielwoche(n), Fest(tag)
bluntness ['blʌntnɪs] blunt	The boss always says what he thinks without trying to be polite. His *bluntness* doesn't make him popular. Last week he spoke to Sally *bluntly*. He simply said, "You're fired."	direkte Art, Offenheit, Grobheit direkt, offen, grob, barsch
rude [ruːd]	very impolite It's *rude* to interrupt a conversation.	unhöflich, plump, grob, rüde
foreigner ['fɒrənə]	somebody from a foreign country	Ausländer(in)
bother (s.b.)	Daddy is busy. Don't *bother* him now. Would it *bother* you if I opened the window?	(jn.) belästigen, stören, ärgern
not altogether	not totally, not completely Arthur is*n't altogether* happy in his new job.	nicht ganz, nicht vollständig
response [rɪ'spɒns]	answer, reaction Abdul filled in lots of application forms, but he didn't get a *response* to any of them.	Antwort; Reaktion

S

characteristic (of)	Ed is often late. It's one of his characteristics. It's *characteristic of* him (to be late).	charakteristisch, typisch (für)
emotional [ɪ'məʊʃənl]	Brian didn't show his emotions. No-one could tell what *emotional* state he was in.	Gefühls-
mental ['mentl]	of, in the mind, opposite of "physical" Whenever Shaun hears the word "home", he sees a *mental* picture of his parents.	geistig, innerlich
adverbial (n.)	another word for "adverb" or "adverbial phrase"	Adverbialbestimmung

18

tramp [træmp]		Landstreicher(in)
collection [kə'lekʃn]	Ed owns a huge *collection* of records.	Sammlung
wound [wuːnd]	Mr Bridges was *wounded* in World War II.	verwunden

Unit 4

Notes on the authors

the Middle East [--'-]	the countries from Egypt to Iran	der Nahe Osten
civil war ['sɪvl'wɔː]		Bürgerkrieg
performer [pə'fɔːmə]	a singer, actor, actress, etc.	Darsteller(in)
mystery ['mɪstərɪ]	The police couldn't solve the *mystery*.	Geheimnis, Rätse
reviewer [rɪ'vjuːə]	a journalist who writes about new books, films, records, TV shows, etc.	Rezensent(in), Kritiker(in)
artist ['ɑːtɪst]	Which *artist* painted the "Mona Lisa"? Joe Green draws pictures for advertisements. He's a commercial *artist*.	(Kunst-)Maler(in) Graphiker(in)

Words and phrases appearing in the poems and narrative texts in Unit 4

adj. = adjective · AE = American English · BE = British English · conj. = conjunction
jm. = jemandem · jn. = jemanden · n. = noun · s.b. = somebody · s.th. = something · v. = verb
→ = look up the word or phrase at the place given

A

abiding [ə'baɪdɪŋ] bleibend
accept sich zufrieden geben mit
account: on account of wegen
accountant → certified
adjustment Regulierung, Einstellung
affection [ə'fekʃn] Zuneigung, Liebe
Ain't they? [eɪnt] (slang) Aren't they?
airlock ['--] Luftschleuse, luftdichter Verschluß
alarm Beunruhigung, Unruhe, Angst
alive [ə'laɪv] lebendig, lebend
all right eben; durchaus; schon
alley ['ælɪ] Gasse, Seitengäßchen
ancient ['eɪnʃənt] uralt
(and) so on [-'--] und so weiter
android ['ændrɔɪd] Androide (künstlicher Mensch)
applause [ə'plɔːz] Beifall
approach [ə'prəʊtʃ] sich nähern
archaic [ɑː'keɪɪk] veraltet
as: as though [-'-] als ob
as to ['æztə] hinsichtlich
ash [æʃ] Asche
aside [ə'saɪd] beiseite, zur Seite
assemble [ə'sembl] sich versammeln
assist [ə'sɪst] helfen
assure [ə'ʃʊə] versichern
atomic [ə'tɒmɪk] atomar, atomisch
atomics [ə'tɒmɪks] Atomantrieb
authority [ɔː'θɒrətɪ] Fachmann
autobiographical [ɔːtəbaɪə'græfɪkl] autobiographisch
automatic (n.) (Selbstlade-)Pistole

B

back (v.) rückwärts fahren
  back and forth [fɔːθ] hin und her
  backyard ['-'-] kleiner Garten hinter dem Haus
banishment ['bænɪʃmənt] Verbannung
bastard ['bɑːstəd] „Schweinehund"
bathe [beɪð] baden
bawl s.b. out [bɔːl] jn. anschnauzen
belly ['belɪ] Bauch
beloved [bɪ'lʌvd] innig geliebt
beneath [bɪ'niːθ] unter, unterhalb
beyond ['-'-] jenseits, über... hinaus
  beyond doubt außer allem Zweifel
Biffo the Bear Figur aus einem Comic
blacken ['blækn] schwarz machen
blame s.th. on s.b. jm. die Schuld geben für etwas
blank [blæŋk] Vordruck, Formular
blend in(to) ineinander übergehen
blind [blaɪnd] blind
blunder ['blʌndə] einen (groben) Fehler machen
board (v.) besteigen, einsteigen
bolt of lightning [bəʊlt] Blitz
bootheel ['buːθiːl] Stiefelabsatz
bottle fruit Obst einmachen, -wecken
bough [baʊ] Ast, Zweig

bow [baʊ] beugen
bowl (of a pipe) (Pfeifen-)Kopf
brassy ['brɑːsɪ] blechern
breath ['breθ] Atem
brief [briːf] kurz
build wachsen
bump off [bʌmp] (slang) „umlegen"
buried ['berɪd] → bury
burst [bɜːst], **it burst, it's burst** ausbrechen
bury ['berɪ] begraben
but: not ... but nicht ..., sondern
by (nahe) bei, neben

C

calm(ly) ruhig, gelassen, still
cane [keɪn] (Spazier-)Stock
care (n.) Kummer, Sorge(n)
cave [keɪv] Höhle
cease [siːs] aufhören
certainty ['---] Gewißheit
certified public accountant (AE) ['sɜː:tɪfaɪdpʌblɪkə'kaʊntənt] amtlich zugelassener Wirtschaftsprüfer
chamber ['tʃeɪmbə] Kammer, Zelle
charity ['tʃærɪtɪ] Wohltätigkeit(sverein, -szweck)
chart [tʃɑːt] skizzieren
cherish ['tʃerɪʃ] schätzen
choose (etwas) vorziehen
chorus ['kɔːrəs] im Chor rufen
cigar [sɪ'gɑː] Zigarre
civilize ['sɪvəlaɪz] zivilisieren
clay [kleɪ] Ton, Erde, Staub
clear your throat sich räuspern
clench ballen, zusammenpressen
cling, **I clung** [klʌŋ], **I've clung (to)** sich klammern, festhalten (an)
cobra ['kəʊbrə] Kobra
companion [kəm'pænjən] Begleiter
confession [kən'feʃn] Geständnis; Beichte
consideration [kənsɪdə'reɪʃn] → take
consult (a list) [kən'sʌlt] (in einer Liste) nachsehen, -schlagen
contemptible [kən'temtəbl] niederträchtig; verächtlich
contract (a disease) [kən'trækt] sich eine Krankheit zuziehen
convict [kən'vɪkt] ab-, verurteilen
coward ['kaʊəd] Feigling
crawl [krɔːl] kriechen
credit ['kredɪt] (AE) (Kurs-) Punktzahl
crush [krʌʃ] zerquetschen, -drücken
curious ['kjʊərɪəs] neugierig

D

daffodil ['dæfədɪl] Osterglocke
damn [dæm] verflucht
darkness Dunkelheit, Finsternis
daylight → in broad daylight

decade ['dekeɪd] Jahrzehnt
declare war (on) jm. den Krieg erklären
deep [diːp] tief
  deep-set ['-'-] tiefliegend
degree → (the) third degree
descend on [dɪ'send] herfallen über
desert (adj.) ['dezət] unbewohnt
despite [dɪ'spaɪt] trotz
destruction [dɪ'strʌkʃn] Vernichtung
dig, I dug [dʌg], **I've dug** (aus-, um-) graben
dirty dreckig, gemein
disease [dɪ'ziːz] Krankheit
distance ['dɪstəns] Entfernung, Ferne
Dopey ['dəʊpɪ] Dummkopf
dossier ['dɒsɪeɪ] (Personal-)Akte
downy ['daʊnɪ] flaumig
draw in (a long) breath [breθ] (tief) einatmen
dress uniform ['-'---] Parade-, Ausgehuniform
drift (fort-, weg-)treiben
drown [draʊn] ertränken
drum (v.) trommeln (auf)

E

eager ['iːgə] begierig, erpicht
earthquake ['ɜːθkweɪk] Erdbeben
ease [iːz] erleichtern, beruhigen
eliminate [ɪ'lɪmɪneɪt] beseitigen
embarrassment [ɪm'bærəsmənt] Verlegenheit
embrace [ɪm'breɪs] umarmen
en suite with [ɒn'swiːt] durch eine Tür verbunden mit
encounter [ɪn'kaʊntə] begegnen
enrich [ɪn'rɪtʃ] bereichern, steigern
entire [ɪn'taɪə] ganz, gesamt
escapist [ɪ'skeɪpɪst] jemand, der vor der Realität flieht
et cetera [ɪt'setrə] etc., usw.
experience (v.) empfinden; erfahren
eyeshade ['aɪʃeɪd] Augenschirm

F

fabric ['fæbrɪk] Gewebe, Stoff
faculty ['fækəltɪ] (AE) Lehrkörper
faint [feɪnt] in Ohnmacht fallen
feel betasten
feverish(ly) ['fiːvrɪʃlɪ] fieberhaft
figure Gestalt, Person
finger out ['fɪŋgə] „herausfingern"
fire away tosen (im Weltraum)
fire down landen (aus dem Weltraum)
flake [fleɪk] (Schnee-)Flocke
flame [fleɪm] Flamme
flash (v.) (auf-)leuchten
flaw [flɔː] Makel, Mangel, Defekt
flicker flackern, flimmern
flood [flʌd] Überflutung
flute [fluːt] (Quer-)Flöte
folk, folks Leute

fool [fu:l] überlisten, täuschen
foolish [ˈfu:lɪʃ] dumm, töricht
for (conj.) denn
  for your own good [--ʹ-ʹ-] in deinem eigenen Interesse
  forever [fəˈrevə] für immer, ewig
  formation: in formation im Verband(sflug)
  forth → back and forth
free (v.) befreien, entlasten
fresh neu, erneut
fringe [frɪndʒ] (äußerer) Rand

G

gallery: art gallery [ˈɑ:tgælərɪ] Kunst-, Gemäldegalerie
gaze at [geɪz] starren auf, anstarren
get in(to) einsteigen, -brechen (in)
glance [glɑ:ns] (flüchtiger) Blick
gleam [gli:m] glitzern, glänzen
glitter [ˈglɪtə] glitzern, schillern
gone: be gone tot sein
good → for your own good
grade: make the grade es schaffen
gratuitous(ly) [grəˈtju:ɪtəslɪ] unentgeltlich, gratis
graveyard [ˈgreɪvjɑ:d] Friedhof
ground floor [ʹ-ʹ-] Erdgeschoß

H

halt [hɔ:lt] einhalten, aufhören
harness [ˈhɑ:nɪs] (Pferde-)Geschirr
health Gesundheit
healthy [ˈhelθɪ] gesund
heartbeat [ˈ--] Herzschlag
Hell! (slang) Verdammt! Verflucht!
  a hell of a lot verdammt viel
heroic [hɪˈrəʊɪk] heldenhaft
hind leg [ˈhaɪndˈleg] Hinterlauf
home (Kinder-)Heim
honeycombed [ˈhʌnɪkəʊmd] mit vielen Zellen (wie eine Honigwabe)
hono(u)r (n., v.) [ˈɒnə] Ehre; (be-)ehren
hood [hʊd] dehnbarer Hals einer Kobra; Kapuze, Kappe
horizon [həˈraɪzn] Horizont
hum [hʌm] summen
hunchbacked [ˈhʌntʃbækt] bucklig
Hungarian [hʌŋˈgeərɪən] Ungar(in)
hush [hʌʃ] Stille, Schweigen

I

icing [ˈaɪsɪŋ] Zuckerguß
ideal [aɪˈdɪəl] Ideal
immense [ɪˈmens] riesig
immensity [ɪˈmensətɪ] Weite
imposing [ɪmˈpəʊzɪŋ] eindrucksvoll
imprison [ɪmˈprɪzn] einsperren
in: in all probability [prɒbəˈbɪlətɪ] aller Wahrscheinlichkeit nach
  in broad daylight am hellichten Tage
  in some small measure bis zu einem gewissen Grad
incurable [ɪnˈkjʊərəbl] unheilbar
indeed [ɪnˈdi:d] in der Tat
indicate [ˈɪndɪkeɪt] hinweisen auf

inexorably [ɪnˈeksrəblɪ] unerbittlich
inherent in [ɪnˈhɪərənt] innewohnend, eingewurzelt in, innerhalb
insane asylum [ɪnˈseɪnəˈsaɪləm] Heil-, Irrenanstalt
institute [ˈɪnstɪtju:t] einleiten
intellectual [ɪntəˈlektʃʊəl] intellektuell
intelligence [ɪnˈtelɪdʒəns] Intelligenz; (geheimer) Nachrichtendienst
interior innengelegen; (der, die, das) Innere
internal innerer, -e, es; privat

K

knife (through) (durch-)schneiden
knot [nɒt] Knoten

L

labo(u)r [ˈleɪbə] schwer arbeiten
landing fields (Anspielung auf eine Rede Churchills aus dem Jahre 1940, in der er sagt: "We shall defend our island, whatever the cost may be, we shall fight . . . .")
late: of late in letzter Zeit
lay eyes on sehen
lean [li:n], **I leaned/I leant** [lent], **I've leant** (sich) lehnen
leap [li:p], **I leaped** [lept, li:pt], **I've leaped** springen
ledge Sims, Gesimse
leisure [ˈleʒə] Muße, Freizeit
lettuce [ˈletɪs] (Kopf-)Salat
liable to [ˈlaɪəbl] wahrscheinlich
lieutenant: first lieutenant [(AE) lu:ˈtenənt, (BE) lefˈtenənt] Oberleutnant
the living die Lebenden
loathsome [ˈləʊðsəm] widerlich
lollipop, lollypop Lutschbonbon
Lord Herr(gott)
lovers Liebespaar(e), Liebende
lowdown on [ʹ--] (slang) Einblick in

M

machine-gun [-ʹ--] Maschinengewehr, -pistole
many: a great many sehr viele
measure → in some small measure
memorial [mɪˈmɔ:rɪəl] Gedächtnis
memory [ˈmemərɪ] Erinnerung; Gedächtnis
mere(ly) [ˈmɪəlɪ] bloß, nur
metal [ˈmetl] metallen, Metall-
metallic [mɪˈtælɪk] metallen
mighty [ˈmaɪtɪ] mächtig, gewaltig
  Mighty Mouse Figur aus einem Comic
miniature [ˈmɪnɪtʃə] Miniatur-, Klein-
minor [ˈmaɪnə] klein, unbedeutend
Mister (AE) = (BE) sir
modesty [ˈmɒdɪstɪ] Bescheidenheit
momentarily [ˈməʊməntrəlɪ] einen Augenblick lang, vorübergehend
mongoose [ˈmɒŋgu:s] Mungo

mongoosexual [mɒŋgʊˈseksjʊəl] „Mungosexuelle(r)"
mongoosism [ˈmɒŋgu:sɪzm] „Mungoismus"
moral [ˈmɒrəl] Moral
motionless [ˈ---] bewegungslos
mound [maʊnd] (Erd-)Hügel
mount (v.) besteigen
mouth Öffnung, Mündung
move (n.) [mu:v] Zug, Schritt

N

natural(ly) natürlich
nearly: not nearly nicht annähernd
neat [ni:t] hübsch, adrett
needle [ˈni:dl] Nadel
Nelson brit. Admiral (1758-1805), der mehrmals verwundet wurde
nibble knabbern, (be-)nagen
nightcap [ˈ--] Nacht-, Schlafmütze
nightgown [ˈnaɪtgaʊn] Nachthemd
no nearer nicht näher
nod nicken
none too good nicht sonderlich gut
nonetheless [--ˈ-] trotzdem
nowadays [ˈnaʊədeɪz] heutzutage
nut [nʌt] Nuß

O

occupant [ˈɒkjʊpənt] Bewohner(in)
offence [əˈfens] Vergehen, Verstoß
on (a matter) in (einer Angelegenheit)
outbound [ˈaʊtbaʊnd] im Abflug
outer [ˈaʊtə] Außen-, äußerer, -e, -es
over and over immer wieder
overcome [---ʹ-] überwältigen
over-excite [---ʹ-] übermäßig aufregen

P

pack (n.) Rudel, Meute
palm [pɑ:m] (Innen-)Handfläche
pantomime [ˈpæntəmaɪm] um Weihnachten aufgeführtes Märchenspiel
pants [pænts] (AE) Unterhose(n), Schlüpfer
parlour game [ˈpɑ:ləgeɪm] Gesellschaftsspiel
pause (v.) innehalten
paw [pɔ:] Pfote, Tatze
peacelike [ˈ--] friedfertig
peripatetic [perɪpəˈtetɪk] umherwandernd; Wanderer
Phi Beta Kappa [ˈfaɪˈbeɪtəˈkæpə] Vereinigung wissenschaftlich hervorragender Akademiker (in den USA)
Phooey on you. [ˈfu:ɪ] Hau ab!
pigeon [ˈpɪdʒɪn] (Brief-)Taube
plain [pleɪn] Ebene, Flachland
plot (eine Verschwörung/einen Anschlag) planen
Pluto [ˈplu:təʊ] Figur aus einem Comic
poppy Mohnblume (wird in England am 11. November, dem Erinnerungstag an den Waffenstillstand nach dem 1. Weltkrieg, verkauft)

146

port(-hole) [′--] Bullauge
possess [pə′zes] besitzen, haben
post [pəʊst] Stellung, Stelle
pound (on) schlagen, hämmern (auf)
pray [preɪ] (an-)beten, anflehen
prayer(s) [preəz] Gebet
pregnant [′pregnənt] schwanger
pre-record [′priːrɪ′kɔːd] vorher (auf Band) aufnehmen
presence [′prezns] Anwesenheit
present (adj.) [′preznt] anwesend
press (v.) er-, bedrücken, bedrängen
probability → in all probability
proceed [prə′siːd] fortfahren
protection [prə′tekʃn] Schutz
pulse [pʌls] pulsieren, pochen
purely rein, ausschließlich
put down (on paper) aufschreiben

Q

queer [kwɪə] seltsam, sonderbar

R

rabbit [′ræbɪt] Kaninchen
ramp [ræmp] Rampe
rat [ræt] Ratte
rate: at any rate [reɪt] jedenfalls
reach 60 60 (Jahre alt) werden
reason Vernunft
record (v.) [rɪ′kɔːd] → pre-record
reflect [rɪ′flekt] nachsinnen
regret [rɪ′gret] bedauern
regular (AE) normal
rehearse [rɪ′hɜːs] üben, proben
remain [rɪ′meɪn] bleiben
remove (from) [rɪ′mjuːv] wegnehmen, entfernen
report (to) sich melden (bei); melden
rest (v.) ruhen, sich ausruhen
resume [rɪ′zjuːm] wieder einnehmen
return zurückbringen
right → all right
rim Rand
ring hallen, erschallen, ertönen
roar (v.) [rɔː] grollen, krachen, lärmen, dröhnen
rounds: make the rounds of die Runde machen; Aufsicht führen
ruin [′rʊɪn] ruinieren, verderben
rumo(u)r [′ruːmə] Gerücht

S

savour [′seɪvə] genießen
scare [skeə] Angst einflößen
scary [′skeərɪ] unheimlich
script (Hand-)Schrift
seamed [siːmd] gezeichnet, zerfurcht
serve dienen, fungieren
Service → Special Service
shaded [′ʃeɪdɪd] schattig, beschattet
shame (v.) beschämen
shape Form, Gestalt, Umriß
shoot dead totschießen
show: by a show of paws durch „Pfotenzeichen"
shower [′ʃaʊə] Dusche
sick krank; verwirrt

sigh [saɪ] seufzen
sight (v.) sichten
silver (adj., n.) silbern; Silber
slide, I slid, I've slid gleiten
smooth [smuːð] ruhig, gleichmäßig
sniff out [′-′-] wittern, riechen
snowy [′snəʊɪ] verschneit
so on → (and) so on
Sol Bezeichnung des Autors für „Sonne"
sometime [′--] irgendwann
sorrow [′sɒrəʊ] Trauer, Leid
sort of like (colloquial) etwa wie
sound of mind and body geistig und körperlich gesund
spare (v.) übrig haben, erübrigen
Special Service [′--′--] Sonderverband, Spezialdienst
spectacles [′spektəklz] Brille
spell (n.) Anfall
splendid [′splendɪd] prächtig
spread [spred], **I spread, I've spread** (sich) ver-, ausbreiten
square (adj.) (vier-)eckig
squirrel [′skwɪrəl] Eichhörnchen
stare [steə] starren; glotzen
startle [′stɑːtl] aufschrecken
steel (adj., n.) [stiːl] stählern; Stahl
steer around [stɪə] um ... herumsteuern, (ver-)meiden
stepfather [′---] Stiefvater
steppingstone [′---] Sprungbrett
stero-shot [′---] Bezeichnung des Autors für „Foto"
still (v.) zur Ruhe kommen
stillness Stille, Ruhe
sting [stɪŋ] Stich, Biß
stop in kurz hereinschauen
storage-locker [′stɔːrɪdʒlɒkə] Lagerschrank
storey [′stɔːrɪ] Stockwerk, Etage
stretch out ausstrecken
stuff [stʌf] (colloquial) Zeug
suffer [′sʌfə] (er-)leiden
summons [′sʌmənz] (Vor-)Ladung
surround [sə′raʊnd] umgeben
suspect [sə′spekt] Verdacht schöpfen, vermuten
suspicion [sə′spɪʃn] Verdacht
swarm [swɔːm] Schwarm
sweep (Dahin-)Fegen, Stürmen
swivel chair [′swɪvl] Drehstuhl

T

tactic [′tæktɪk] Taktik
take into consideration bedenken
tear (n.) [tɪə] Träne
tear off abreißen
tension [′tenʃn] Spannung
thaw [θɔː] schmelzen, auftauen
theft [θeft] Diebstahl
theory [′θɪərɪ] Theorie
There's jobs. (slang) There are jobs.
think of ... as betrachten ... als
(the) third degree Folterverhör
though: as though [-′-] als ob
thought (n.) Gedanke, Überlegung
thread [θred] ein-, durchfädeln; durchdringen, sich winden durch
threaten [′θretn] (be-)drohen
throng [θrɒŋ] (Menschen-)Menge

thrown in dreingegeben, gratis
thrust [θrʌst], **it thrust, it's thrust** heraustreten
thunder [′θʌndə] Donner
tight (an-)gespannt; straff
tightly eng, fest
tilted [′tɪltɪd] schräg
torture [′tɔːtʃə] Folter
toward [tə′wɔːd] auf ... zu
tracker dog [′---] Spürhund
treason [′triːzn] (Hoch-, Landes-)Verrat
tremble [′trembl] zittern
triumph [′traɪəmf] Triumph
truthful(ly) wahrheitsgemäß
try on anprobieren
try s.b. jn. vor Gericht stellen
turn yourself in sich freiwillig stellen
twist [twɪst] (ver-)drehen
two-storey zweistöckig

U

unite [juː′naɪt] sich zusammentun
universe [′juːnɪvɜːs] (Welt-)All
unsteady unsicher, schwankend
upwards [′--] aufwärts, nach oben
urge [ɜːdʒ] Drang, Trieb, Lust

V

vast [vɑːst] groß, unermeßlich
venom [′venəm] (Schlangen-)Gift
very: at this very moment gerade/eben jetzt
view (v.) ansehen, betrachten
vow [vaʊ] schwören, geloben

W

wagon [′wægən] (AE) Wagen
wagon box (AE) (Wagen-)Ladefläche
walkway [′--] (Lauf-)Gang, Steg
wasted [′weɪstɪd] verbraucht
weakness Schwäche
wedding-cake [′---] Hochzeitskuchen
well-wisher [′---] Gratulant(in)
West Point [′-′-] U.S.-Militärakademie
What of ... ? Wie stand es um ... ?
will (n.) Testament
wolf, wolves [wʊlf, wʊlvz] Wolf, Wölfe
wondrous [′wʌndrəs] wundersam
Woolton [′wʊltən] Ort bei Liverpool in der Nähe des Flughafens
would (speak) pflegte zu (sprechen)
wrinkled [′rɪŋkld] faltig, runzlig
wristwatch [′--] Armbanduhr

Y

yarn [jɑːn] (miteinander) schwatzen
yellow feige
yer [jə] nachlässige Aussprache von "you"

List of words

1 A = Unit 1, Acquisition · 2 Ex = Unit 2, Exercises · 3 S = Unit 3, Summary ·
4 A/T = Unit 4, Acquisition/Text
adj. = adjective · adv. = adverb · conj. = conjunction · n. = noun · prep. = preposition
s.b. = somebody · s.th. = something · v. = verb

A

above (adj.) 1 Ex
about: concerned about 3 A
accurate 3 A
accusation 4 A/T
accuse s.b. of 1 A
accustomed to 2 T 2
additional 4 A/T
adequate 1 T
adverbial (n.) 4 S
advisable 2 A
adviser (on) 3 A
affect 1 A
agent 1 A
aid 4 A/T
alcohol 3 T
alien (adj., n.) 2 T 2
alone: let alone 2 A
alternative (adj.) 3 A
altogether: not altogether 4 Ex
aluminium 3 A
amazement 2 T 2
amuse 4 A/T
analyse 4 A/T
announce 1 A
anorak 3 Ex
anyway 2 T 2
apart from 2 A
appoint 1 A
appreciation 4 A/T
Arab (adj., n.) 3 A
Arabic 2 A
arrange 2 A
as: as a matter of fact 2 Ex
   as I say 2 Ex
ask: a lot to ask (of s.b) 3 Ex
at: be shocked at 3 A
atmosphere 4 A/T
attractive 1 T
author 4 A/T
aware of/that 3 A

B

back to normal 3 A
ballot paper 1 Ex
barrel 3 A
BBC 2 A
be: be accustomed to 2 T 2
   be aware of/that 3 A
   be drunk 1 Ex
   be obliged to 1 A
   be shocked (at) 3 A
   be supposed to 1 A
   be to 1 A
   be willing to 1 A
beauty 4 A/T
become aware of/that 3 A
believe in 3 A
below (adv., prep.) 3 A
better: know better (than to) 1 Ex
blackout 3 A
blame (n.) 1 Ex
   blame s.b. (for) 1 Ex
blunt 4 Ex
bluntness 4 Ex
boot 3 T
bother (v.) 4 Ex
bright 3 T
broad 2 A
bunk 3 T
business 2 T 2
but: last but not least 2 A
by the way 3 T
by-election 1 A

C

C (centigrade) 3 A
Cabinet 1 A
campaign (n., v.) 1 A
candidate 1 A
can't help it if 1 Ex
capita: per capita 3 A
cassette 1 Ex
   cassette recorder 1 Ex
centigrade 3 A
characteristic (adj.) 4 S
characterization 4 A/T
characterize 4 A/T
chat (n.) 4 Ex
cheerful 3 T
cheque: traveller's cheque 1 Ex

circumstances 1 T
civil: civil servant 1 A
   civil service 2 A
class: working-class (adj., n.) 1 T
climax 4 A/T
coal 1 T
   coal-field 3 A
Cockney (adj., n.) 2 A
coke 3 A
comic (adj.) 4 A/T
committee 1 T
Common Market 1 A
Commons: the (House of) Commons 1 A
company director 1 T
concerned (about) 3 A
conference 1 A
conflict (n., v.) 1 T
connotation 4 A/T
conscience 1 T
conservation 3 A
Conservative (adj., adv., n.) 1 A
conserve 3 A
constant 3 A
constituency 1 A
consumption 3 A
contain 4 A/T
contribute (to) 4 A/T
convert (into) 3 A
country: developing country 3 A
copy (n.) 3 Ex
correspond (to/with) 4 A/T
create 4 A/T
crisis, crises 3 A
critical 4 A/T
cross (n.) 1 Ex
crude oil 3 A
culture 2 A

D

dawn 3 T
day: polling day 1 A
   the other day 2 T 2
debate 1 T
deck 3 T

148

deduction 3 S
defence 1 A
degree 3 A
democratic 1 A
dependence (on) 3 A
detailed 1 T
developing (country) 3 A
diagram 3 A
director: company director 1 T
discipline 1 A
division 4 A/T
do (miles) per (gallon) 3 A
dot 4 A/T
down: turn down 1 A
drill (n., v.) 3 A
drive (a machine) 3 A
drunk: be/get drunk 1 Ex
duty: be off duty 3 T
   sense of duty 1 S

E

economical 3 A
effective 1 A
efficient 3 A
elect 1 A
election: by-election 1 A
   general election 1 A
element 4 A/T
emotional 4 S
end: open-ended 4 A/T
energy 3 A
engineer 3 T
engineering 3 T
environment 3 A
envy 3 T
exhaustible 3 A
explicit 4 A/T
exposition 4 A/T

F

fable 4 A/T
fact: as a matter of fact 2 Ex
factor 3 A
fairy-story 4 A/T
favourite (n.) 1 A
fear 3 T
-featured 3 T
federal 1 A

festival 4 Ex
fiction 4 A/T
   science fiction 4 A/T
   work of fiction 4 A/T
field 3 A
fission: nuclear fission 3 A
fist 3 T
flash of lightning 3 A
flashback 4 A/T
food: frozen food 1 A
foot 4 A/T
for: blame s.b. for 1 Ex
   reproach s.b. for 1 Ex
foreigner 2 Ex
form (v.) 3 A
fossil fuels 3 A
French: the French 1 Ex
from: apart from 2 A
   prevent from ... ing 3 A
frozen food 1 A
fuel: fuel oil 3 A
   fossil fuels 3 A
function 4 A/T
fusion: nuclear fusion 3 A

G

gap 2 Ex
gas, gases 3 A
   gas-field 3 A
   natural gas 3 A
general election 1 A
generate 3 T
geologist 3 T
get: get accustomed to 2 T 2
   get (done) 1 A
   get drunk 1 Ex
   get the picture 1 Ex
ghetto 3 A
gradual(ly) 2 A
graduate 3 T
gravestone 2 A
group: pressure group 1 T
grow (in) 2 A
growth 3 A

H

hand: shake hands (with) 1 A
happen to 1 A
heat (v.) 3 A
heating 3 A

helmet 3 T
help: can't help it if 1 Ex
here: Look here. 1 Ex
hero, heroine 3 T
hesitate 2 Ex
hitch-hike 2 Ex
house: the House of Commons 1 A
   the House of Lords 1 A
   the Houses of Parliament 1 A
household 3 A
How can/shall I put it? 1 Ex

I

I'd rather 3 Ex
if: If ... should 2 A
   can't help it if 1 Ex
image 4 A/T
imitate 4 A/T
implicit 4 A/T
import (n., v.) 3 A
importance 1 A
impression 2 A
in: in no way 2 S
   in (this) respect 2 A
   believe in 3 A
   involve in 3 A
   1 in (5) 2 A
inadequate 1 T
incident 3 T
increase (n., v.) 3 A
industrial 3 A
industrialized 3 A
ineffective 1 A
inefficient 3 A
inexhaustible 3 A
insist (on) 1 A
install 3 A
insulation 3 A
intention 3 S
interpret 4 A/T
interpretation 4 A/T
interviewer 1 A
into: convert into 3 A
   research into 1 T
   turn into 1 A
intransitive 2 S
inversion 2 S
invest 2 Ex
involve (in) 3 A
(the) Irish 2 A
ironic(al) 4 A/T

irony 4 A/T
Israeli (adj., n.) 3 A
issue 1 A
it: There's s.th. in it. 2 Ex

J

judge (n.) 1 T

K

keep: keep ... ing 1 A
key (adj.) 1 A
know better (than to) 1 Ex
knowledge 2 A
    working knowledge 2 T 2

L

Labour (adj., adv., n.) 1 A
language: native language 2 A
    second language 2 A
last but not least 2 A
laundry 3 Ex
leaf, leaves 3 T
leaflet 1 A
least: last but not least 2 A
leave (n.) 3 T
lend 1 Ex
lengthen 2 Ex
let alone 2 A
Liberal (adj., adv., n.) 1 A
library 1 T
light (v.) 2 T 2
lightning 3 A
    flash of lightning 3 A
likely 1 A
limerick 2 T 3
limit (to) 4 A/T
loneliness 3 T
lonely 3 T
look: Look (here). 1 Ex
loot 3 A
lord 1 A
    the (House of) Lords 1 A
lot: a lot to ask (of s.b.)
    3 Ex
love (n.) 3 T

M

manufacture 3 A
market: Common Market 1 A
matter: as a matter of fact 2 Ex
    subject matter 4 A/T
may 1 A
measure 3 A
Member of Parliament 1 A
mental 4 S
mess up 1 Ex
metaphor 4 A/T
metre 4 A/T
midnight 3 T
mine (n.) 1 T
miner 1 T
minister 1 A
    Prime Minister 1 A
moreover 1 A
most (adv.) 2 T 2
move: move on 4 A/T
    move up 3 Ex
MP 1 A
mud 3 T
mutter 2 T 2
my: of my own 3 A

N

narrative text 4 A/T
native language 2 A
natural gas 3 A
network 1 A
neutral 2 A
newsreader 2 A
no: no sooner ... than 1 A
    in no way 2 S
noon 3 T
nor 3 A
normal: back to normal 3 A
Norwegian 3 T
not: not altogether 4 Ex
novel 3 T
nuclear 1 A
    nuclear fission 3 A
    nuclear fusion 3 A
    nuclear power station 1 A

O

obligation 1 A
obliged: be obliged to 1 A

obstacle 2 A
of: of (my) own 3 A
    accuse s.b. of 1 A
    aware of 3 A
    a lot to ask of s.b. 3 Ex
    remind s.b. of 3 T
    run out of 3 A
off: be off duty 3 T
    take (time) off 3 T
oil: oil-field 3 A
    oil rig 3 A
    crude oil 3 A
    fuel oil 3 A
omission 2 S
on: adviser on 3 A
    dependence on 3 A
    move on 4 A/T
    research on 1 T
one in (five) 2 A
open-ended 4 A/T
opinion poll 1 A
opponent 1 A
opposition 1 A
other: the other day
    2 T 2
out: run out (of) 3 A
over: take over 2 A
own: of (my) own 3 A

P

pale 3 T
panic 3 T
paper: ballot paper 1 Ex
paperback (adj., n.) 3 T
parallel 4 A/T
paraphrase 1 Ex
parliament 1 A
    the Houses of Parliament
    1 A
    Member of Parliament 1 A
parody 4 A/T
partly 1 T
party 1 A
path 3 Ex
pension 1 A
per: per capita 3 A
    do (miles) per (gallon) 3 A
perfect 2 T 2
phrasal verb 1 Ex
pick up 2 T 2
picture: get the picture 1 Ex

pipeline 3 A
plastic (n.) 3 A
platform 3 T
playful 4 A/T
PM 1 A
poet 4 A/T
poetry 4 A/T
politician 1 A
poll: opinion poll 1 A
polling day 1 A
Portuguese 2 A
power 1 A
   (nuclear) power station 1 A
prepositional phrase 2 Ex
pressure group 1 T
prevent (from ... ing) 3 A
Prime Minister 1 A
print 4 A/T
prisoner 3 T
profit 1 A
profitable 3 A
proverb 2 Ex
pump 3 T
pursue 3 A
put: put right 3 Ex
   put up 3 Ex
   put up with 1 A
   How can/shall I put it? 1 Ex

R

radioactive 3 A
rather: I'd rather 3 Ex
record 1 T
recorder: cassette recorder 1 Ex
recount 1 A
recycle 3 A
refine 3 A
region 2 A
regional 2 A
remarkable 2 A
remind s.b. of/to 3 T
report (v.) 1 A
represent 1 A
reproach (n.) 1 Ex
   reproach s.b. for 1 Ex
republic 1 A
research (on/into) 1 T
respect: in (this) respect 2 A

respond (to) 3 Ex
response 4 Ex
rhyme (n.) 2 T 3
rhyme (with) (v.) 2 A
rhythm 4 A/T
rig: oil rig 3 A
right: put right 3 Ex
rise 3 A
rude 4 Ex
run out (of) 3 A

S

sample 3 T
satire 4 A/T
say: as I say 2 Ex
scan (v.) 2 T 3
scheme 4 A/T
science fiction 4 A/T
scientist 1 A
search (for) (n., v.) 3 A
seat: take a seat 1 A
second language 2 A
section 4 A/T
sense of duty 1 S
servant: civil servant 1 A
service: civil service 2 A
setting 4 A/T
shake hands (with) 1 A
shift 3 T
shock (v.) 3 A
short story 4 A/T
should: If ... should 2 A
silence 3 T
simile 4 A/T
sky 3 T
slang 2 A
slight(ly) 2 A
smell (n.) 3 T
snowstorm 3 A
socialist 1 A
soft 2 T 2
solar 3 A
solution 4 A/T
something: There's something in it. 2 Ex
sooner: no sooner ... than 1 A
sour 3 A
standard (adj.) 2 A
stanza 4 A/T
station: (nuclear) power station 1 A
status 2 A

still 4 A/T
store (v.) 3 A
story: fairy-story 4 A/T
   short story 4 A/T
style 3 Ex
subject matter 4 A/T
summarize 4 A/T
supply 3 A
supposed: be supposed to 1 A
surface 3 A
suspense 4 A/T
symbolic 4 A/T

T

take: take a seat 1 A
   take (time) off 3 T
   take over 2 A
taxi 2 A
taxpayer 1 A
technological 3 A
tense (adj.) 3 T
text: narrative text 4 A/T
than: know better than to 1 Ex
   no sooner ... than 1 A
the: the French 1 Ex
   the Irish 2 A
   the other day 2 T 2
   The thing is, ... 2 Ex
theme 4 A/T
There's s.th. in it. 2 Ex
thing: The thing is, ... 2 Ex
thoroughly 2 A, 4 A/T
tidal 3 A
tides 3 A
time: take (time) off 3 T
title 1 A
to: accustomed to 2 T 2
   back to normal 3 A
   be obliged to 1 A
   be supposed to 1 A
   be to 1 A
   be willing to 1 A
   contribute to 4 A/T
   correspond to 4 A/T
   happen to 1 A
   limit to 4 A/T
   remind s.b. to 3 T
   respond to 3 Ex
   turn to 1 A
   You're welcome to. 3 Ex

tone 4 A/T
total (n.) 3 A
trade union 1 A
transfer 3 T
transitive 2 S
transport (v.) 3 A
traveller 1 Ex
   traveller's cheque 1 Ex
turbine 3 A
turn 1 A
   turn down 1 A
   turn to/into 1 A

U

unaware of/that 3 A
unimaginable 3 T
union: trade union 1 A
unlike 1 T
unlikely 1 A
unpredictable 3 A
up: mess up 1 Ex
   move up 3 Ex
   pick up 2 T 2

put up 3 Ex
   put up with 1 A
uranium 3 A
urgent 3 A

V

vary 2 A
verb: phrasal verb 1 Ex
verse 2 T 3
vote (n.) 1 A
voter 1 A
vowel 2 A

W

waste (n.) 3 A
way: by the way 3 T
   in no way 2 S
weathered 3 T
week: the other week 2 T 2
welcome: You're welcome to. 3 Ex
Welsh (n.) 2 A

western 2 A
willing: be willing to 1 A
with: correspond with 4 A/T
   put up with 1 A
   rhyme with 2 A
   shake hands with 1 A
within 2 A
wop 3 T
work (n.) 4 A/T
   work of fiction 4 A/T
working-class (adj., n.) 1 T
   working knowledge 2 T 2
world-wide 2 A
would: I'd rather 3 Ex

Y

yawn 3 T
yet (adv.) 2 T 2, (conj.) 2 A
you: You're welcome to. 3 Ex

Z

Zambian (adj., n.) 3 Ex

Deutsch-englische Übersetzungsstücke

Unit 1 Eine Nachwahl

Harald Schmidt ist wieder einmal zu Besuch bei seinem Freund Peter Garret, der in der Nähe Londons wohnt. Harald interessiert sich sehr für Politik und freut sich, daß während seines Aufenthaltes in England eine Nachwahl stattfinden wird. Er bittet Peter gleich am ersten Abend, ihm das britische Wahlsystem zu erklären.

Peter: Spätestens alle fünf Jahre werden in Großbritannien allgemeine Parlamentswahlen abgehalten, in denen die Abgeordneten des Unterhauses gewählt werden. Das ganze Land ist in 635 Wahlkreise mit durchschnittlich 60.000 Wählern aufgeteilt. In jedem dieser Wahlkreise wird ein Kandidat gewählt, der dann dieses Gebiet im Parlament vertritt. Es gewinnt der Kandidat, der die meisten Stimmen erhält, wobei die Mehrheit von einer Stimme ausreicht.

Harald: Das bedeutet aber doch, daß die Wähler, die die Kandidaten der anderen Parteien gewählt haben, mit ihrer politischen Meinung dann gar nicht im Unterhaus vertreten sind, oder? Und die kleineren Parteien haben offensichtlich nur geringe Chancen, Sitze im Unterhaus zu gewinnen.

Peter: Du denkst sicher an euer Wahlsystem in Deutschland. Auch hier in Großbritannien gibt es Leute, die ein Verhältniswahlrecht vorziehen würden. Vor allem die Mitglieder der Liberalen Partei sind der Meinung, daß jede Stimme zählen sollte. Wenn man sich die Wahlergebnisse vom Oktober 1974 ansieht, weiß man warum. Damals erhielten die Liberalen 18,3% der Gesamtstimmenzahl, aber nur 2,1% der Unterhaussitze! Und vergiß nicht, der Abgeordnete soll nach Ansicht der meisten Leute den ganzen Wahlkreis, also alle Wähler, in Westminster vertreten und nicht nur die Interessen seiner Partei.

Harald: Warum ist in eurem Wahlkreis eine Nachwahl notwendig?

Peter: Unser bisheriger Abgeordneter starb vor acht Wochen, und nun wird am nächsten Donnerstag die Nachwahl sein. Sechs Kandidaten werden versuchen, die Wahl zu gewinnen, aber nur drei haben nach Meinung der meisten Experten eine echte Chance: der neue Mann der Konservativen und die beiden Kandidaten der Labourpartei und der Liberalen.

Peters ältere Schwester Judy ist Wahlkampfhelferin der Konservativen Partei. Sie erzählt Harald, wie sie für ihren Kandidaten um Stimmen wirbt.

Judy: Nun, wenn wir von der Schule heimgehen, verteilen wir Flugblätter und hängen Plakate in den Geschäften aus. Wir haben sehr hübsche Aufkleber, die wir unseren Freunden geben. Manchmal helfen wir auch im Büro unseres Kandidaten.

Harald: Erzähl doch mal, Judy, was macht euer Kandidat während des Wahlkampfes?

Judy: Mr Peters muß schwer arbeiten. Fast jeden Abend muß er auf einer Versammlung sprechen. Während der Hauptgeschäftszeit stellt er sich gerne vor die Geschäfte, spricht die Leute an und erklärt ihnen seine Ansichten über die wichtigsten Themen. Häufig geht er auch in die Häuser und Wohnungen der Leute, um dort mit ihnen zu diskutieren. Jede Woche gibt er eine Pressekonferenz. Sein Ziel ist es natürlich, daß man ihn kennt und sich an ihn erinnert. Wie jeder andere Kandidat auch, will er, daß sein Name so oft wie möglich in den Zeitungen gedruckt wird. Morgen könnt ihr ein Interview mit ihm in der Zeitung lesen.

Am Abend des Wahltages waren Harald und Peter am Rathaus, um so schnell wie möglich das Wahlergebnis zu erfahren. Dort trafen sie Judy und Mr Garret, der ihnen sagte, daß sie spätestens um 11 Uhr zu Hause sein sollten. Judy war sehr müde, da sie den ganzen Nachmittag über ältere Wähler der Konservativen Partei, die sonst vielleicht zu Hause geblieben wären, zu den Wahllokalen gefahren hatte. Die Wahllokale, die um 7 Uhr geöffnet worden waren, wurden um 10 Uhr abends geschlossen, und die Urnen wurden ins Rathaus gebracht, wo man die Stimmen zählte. Da die Ergebnisse sehr knapp waren, mußten die Stimmen noch einmal gezählt werden, bevor das Endergebnis bekanntgegeben werden konnte. Es war schon recht spät, sicher später als 11 Uhr, als plötzlich einige anfingen, Beifall zu klatschen. Der Wahlsieger war der Kandidat der Konservativen und neue Abgeordnete John Peters.

Unit 2   a) Schüleraustausch

In Haralds Klasse besprechen die Schüler mit ihrem Englischlehrer, Herrn Schneider, was sie während des kommenden Besuchs der Austauschschüler ihrer englischen Partnerschule unternehmen könnten.

Herr S.: In den nächsten Tagen möchte ich einen Brief an unsere englischen Freunde schreiben und ihnen mitteilen, was wir während ihres Besuchs unternehmen wollen. Ihr sollt mir daher Vorschläge machen. Denkt auch daran, was uns im letzten Jahr nicht so gefallen hat.

Thomas: Wie wär's, wenn wir wieder ein Fußballspiel gegen sie austragen würden? Letztes Jahr war's doch großartig, nicht?
Robert: Das stimmt. Aber das Spiel wäre für unsere englischen Freunde viel schöner gewesen, wenn wir mehr Zuschauer gehabt hätten.
Mark: Richtig. Wenn uns der Direktor am Vormittag spielen ließe, könnten alle Schüler zusehen.
Gisela: Aber ein Fußballspiel ist doch nicht so wichtig. Mir hat das letzte Mal nicht gefallen, daß wir so wenig Gelegenheit hatten, mit den Besuchern Englisch zu sprechen. Der Austausch hat nur dann einen Vorteil für uns, wenn wir viel Englisch sprechen können.
Sabine: Wenn du mich fragst, so halte ich es für das Wichtigste, daß die Engländer bei unseren Familien wohnen. Denn wenn sie nicht bei ihren Freunden wohnen, können sie nie feststellen, wie das Leben in einem anderen Land wirklich ist.
Georg: Du hast völlig recht. Aber da gibt es ja keine Schwierigkeiten bei uns. Ich möchte einen Radausflug vorschlagen.
Herr S.: Das ist keine schlechte Idee. Wir hatten schon im vorigen Jahr so etwas vor. Wenn das Wetter nicht so schlecht gewesen wäre, hätten wir schon damals einen Ausflug gemacht. Falls wir nicht genügend Fahrräder haben, könnten wir bei Petras Vater einige ausleihen, nicht wahr, Petra?
Petra: Sicher. Wir dürfen aber nicht vergessen, daß die englischen Schüler auch an unserem Unterricht teilnehmen sollten. Im letzten Jahr waren sie nur einmal in unserer Klasse. Sie sollten diesmal öfter zu uns kommen.
Martina: Klar. Aber die Hauptsache ist, daß wir Kontakte knüpfen und Freundschaften schließen. Wenn wir das erreichen wollen, müssen wir auch einmal mit ihnen in die Disco gehen.
Herr S.: Ihr habt einige gute Vorschläge gemacht, aber ich glaube, wir müssen uns morgen noch einmal darüber unterhalten. Überlegt euch bis morgen bitte noch weitere Vorschläge.

b) Hochsprache und Dialekt

Abgesehen vom Walisischen und Gälischen, den ursprünglichen Sprachen der Waliser, Schotten und Iren, gibt es in Großbritannien, wie in anderen Ländern auch, Dialekte und regionale Akzente.

Die Dialekte unterscheiden sich von der Hochsprache im Wortschatz, in der Grammatik und vor allem in der Aussprache. Da die meisten Menschen, die einen breiten Dialekt sprechen, in ländlichen Gegenden leben, verwundert es nicht, daß vor allem der Wortschatz des bäuerlichen Lebens in den Dialektgebieten sehr verschieden ist. In bezug auf die Grammatik unterscheiden sich die Dialekte vom

„Standard English" häufig im Gebrauch der Pronomina, vor allem in den westlichen Teilen Englands. Heute allerdings sprechen immer weniger Briten einen Dialekt, da Fernsehen und Radio „Standard English" in jedes Haus bringen.

Cockney, in London gesprochen, ist der berühmteste britische Dialekt. Wenn auch nicht alle Londoner Arbeiter ein ausgeprägtes Cockney-Englisch sprechen, haben doch viele eine Aussprache und einen Wortschatz, die einen Fremden oft an seinen eigenen Englischkenntnissen zweifeln lassen, wenn er z. B. zum ersten Mal einen Londoner Polizisten um eine Auskunft bittet oder mit einem Taxifahrer eine Unterhaltung anfangen will.

Im Gegensatz zu Deutschland glaubt man in Großbritannien, daß es für gebildete Angehörige der Mittelschicht nicht angebracht sei, mit einem regionalen Akzent zu sprechen. Für viele Briten ist es nämlich immer noch von Bedeutung, ob jemand der Arbeiterklasse oder der Mittelschicht angehört. Ein leichter Akzent mag wohl noch als erträglich gelten, ein ausgeprägter Akzent muß aber nach Meinung dieser Leute abgelegt werden, wenn jemand eine Spitzenposition bei den Streitkräften oder im Verwaltungsdienst erringen oder als Arzt oder Rechtsanwalt Anerkennung finden will. Für Leute mit solchen Berufszielen ist es gut, wenn sie die Sprechweise der Nachrichtensprecher im Fernsehen und im Rundfunk annehmen. Je weiter jemand oben auf der gesellschaftlichen Stufenleiter steht, desto wahrscheinlicher verwendet er diese Form des Englischen, die als BBC-Englisch bekanntgeworden ist. Im Unterschied zur Mehrheit der Deutschen, die sowohl Hochdeutsch wie auch einen Dialekt sprechen, ist es für einen Briten sehr ungewöhnlich, sich zu Hause im Dialekt zu unterhalten, aber im Beruf oder in der Öffentlichkeit „Standard English" zu verwenden.

Unit 3   a) Energie – Ein Hauptproblem unserer Zeit

In den letzten Jahren hat es immer wieder Augenblicke gegeben, in denen den Menschen bewußt wurde, was für eine ungeheuer wichtige Rolle die Energie in ihrem Leben spielt. So waren im Jahr 1977 neun Millionen New Yorker 25 Stunden lang ohne Strom. Das bedeutete beispielsweise, daß die Züge der Untergrundbahn in den Tunnels stehenblieben, daß die Aufzüge nicht mehr weiterfuhren und die Leute 25 Stunden darin bleiben mußten. Oder 1973: Als während des arabisch-israelischen Krieges die arabischen Ölländer ihr Öl nicht mehr an bestimmte Länder verkaufen wollten, war in diesen Ländern Benzin eine Zeitlang sehr knapp. In Deutschland z. B. durften am Sonntag keine Privatautos fahren. Die leeren Autobahnen und Straßen boten ein ganz und gar ungewohntes Bild und machten, wenigstens für eine kurze Zeit, jedem deutlich, wie sehr der gewohnte Lebensstil in einem modernen Industriestaat von der Energie abhängig ist.

Wenn auch die Menschen, sobald die Krise vorüber war, recht schnell wieder zu ihren früheren Gewohnheiten zurückkehrten, blieb doch bei vielen der Eindruck, daß die Energieversorgung eines der wichtigsten Probleme der achtziger und neunziger Jahre sein würde. Auch wegen der Unfälle in den Kernkraftwerken während der letzten Jahre wird das Thema Energie in der Öffentlichkeit immer häufiger diskutiert.

Die zentrale Frage dieser Diskussion lautet: Was kann man tun, wenn einerseits der Energieverbrauch ständig steigt und andererseits die Energiereserven nicht unerschöpflich sind? Alle Experten sind der Meinung, daß die Weltreserven an Kohle, Gas und Öl eines Tages zu Ende sein werden. Allerdings sind die Fachleute uneins über den Zeitpunkt, zu dem die Reserven erschöpft sein werden, da man nicht genau vorhersagen kann, wie viele Reserven noch entdeckt werden. Daher ist die Antwort auf die zweite Frage, welche alternativen Energiequellen gefunden werden können, von großer Bedeutung. Und schließlich sollte nicht vergessen werden, daß die Energieversorgung auch von der politischen und wirtschaftlichen Entwicklung der ganzen Welt abhängt.

In diesem Jahrhundert wurde ungefähr so viel Energie verbraucht wie in den 19 Jahrhunderten zuvor. Es stieg aber nicht nur der Gesamtverbrauch. In den Industrieländern wie auch in den Entwicklungsländern verbraucht jeder einzelne von Jahr zu Jahr mehr Energie.

Welche Möglichkeiten zur Lösung des Energieproblems gibt es? Eine Möglichkeit besteht darin, neue Lagerstätten der traditionellen Energiequellen zu suchen. Dies aber wird immer schwieriger und teurer. Wichtige Faktoren sind auch die Transportkosten und, in den letzten Jahren zunehmend, die möglichen Gefahren für die Umwelt.

Die zweite Möglichkeit ist die Entwicklung neuer Energiequellen, von denen die Atomenergie und die Sonnenenergie nach unserem heutigen Wissen die bedeutendsten sind. Diese neuen Energiequellen haben Vor- und Nachteile. Die Energiegewinnung aus Atomkraft verursacht zwar, verglichen mit der Kohle, keinen Rauch und ist auch billiger, aber das Problem der Entsorgung und die Sicherheitsfrage sind enorme Nachteile. Obwohl die Sonnenenergie keinerlei Probleme für die Umwelt bringt, kann sie nicht in allen Gebieten der Welt effektiv verwendet werden, und die dafür nötigen Anlagen sind ziemlich teuer.

Natürlich gibt es noch die Möglichkeit, Energie zu sparen und z. B. die Isolierung der Büros und Wohnhäuser zu verbessern oder verbrauchte Materialien wiederzuverwenden. Viele Menschen sind der Ansicht, daß es Aufgabe der Regierungen und der großen Konzerne sei, ihre Energiepolitik zu überdenken. Sie vergessen aber dabei, daß alle Möglichkeiten der Energieeinsparung verfolgt werden müssen und daß jeder seinen eigenen Beitrag zu leisten hat, wenn es auch in Zukunft ausreichend Energie geben soll.

b) Ein Interview: Arbeit auf einer Bohrinsel in der Nordsee

(Dieser Abschnitt und das folgende Interview brauchen nicht übersetzt zu werden, da die Übersetzungsaufgabe darin besteht, aus dem Interview einen Zeitungsbericht in der indirekten Rede zu schreiben.)

Reporter: Wie lange arbeiten Sie schon hier?
Ingenieur: Ich arbeite schon 3 Monate hier, aber es ist sehr unterschiedlich, da die meisten von uns häufig von einer Bohrinsel zur anderen versetzt werden. Sie sollten dabei bedenken, daß die Aufstiegsmöglichkeiten in der Ölindustrie groß sind. Viele akzeptieren daher häufigere Wechsel.
Reporter: Erzählen Sie mir doch bitte etwas über Ihre Arbeitszeit.
Geologe: Wir arbeiten zwei Wochen auf der Insel, dann werden wir vom Hubschrauber wieder an Land gebracht und haben dort zwei Wochen Urlaub. Auf der Insel sind die Schichten so eingeteilt, daß die meisten von 12 Uhr nachts bis 12 Uhr mittags – oder umgekehrt – arbeiten.
Bohrschlammspezialist:
Das trifft allerdings nicht für alle zu. Erst gestern mußte ich 24 Stunden ununterbrochen arbeiten. Es war eine schwierige Lage eingetreten, da der Bohrmeißel zu heiß geworden war. Aber wir schafften es. Wir sind ein Team, jeder gibt sein Bestes, weil jeder darauf angewiesen ist, daß die anderen gut arbeiten und keine Fehler machen.
Reporter: Welches sind die größten Schwierigkeiten?
Geologe: Zunächst möchte ich die immer gleiche Routine nennen, die uns sehr auf die Nerven geht. Am ersten oder zweiten Tag nach der Rückkehr von Land unterhält man sich noch über den letzten Urlaub, aber dann gibt es nichts mehr, worüber man reden kann. Alkohol ist auf der Insel auch nicht erlaubt. Da kommt es dann schon vor, daß einige eine Rauferei anfangen.
Bohrmeister: Es gibt auch noch andere Schwierigkeiten. Am Anfang fühlt sich jeder als ein Held der Technik, der einer dankbaren Nation das dringend benötigte Öl verschafft. Wenn dann aber 6 Monate, 12 Monate gebohrt und kein Öl entdeckt wird, verliert er dieses Gefühl sehr schnell. Ich kannte einen Geologen, der mehr als 5 Jahre nach Öl suchte, ohne jemals einen Fund zu machen, der eine Erschließung wert gewesen wäre.
Ingenieur: Wenn von Schwierigkeiten gesprochen wird, darf man nicht vergessen, daß die Frauen oder Freundinnen der Männer die lange Abwesenheit nicht mögen. Für sie besteht das Leben eben aus mehr als einem hohen Verdienst.
Reporter: Was fürchten Sie auf Ihrer Bohrinsel?
Bohrmeister: Einen plötzlichen Öl- oder Gasausbruch. Erst vor kurzem gab es in einem norwegischen Ölfeld einen solchen Ausbruch, bei dem sich

	Tausende von Tonnen Rohöl in die Nordsee ergossen und die Bohrinsel einer ungeheuren Feuergefahr aussetzten.
Geologe:	Sicherlich nicht so gefährlich, aber für uns alle schlimm genug ist es, wenn ein Sturm verhindert, daß die Hubschrauber landen oder ein Boot die Insel erreichen kann. Oft müssen wir dann auf unseren Landurlaub warten. Wir brauchen zwar keine Angst zu haben, daß unsere Vorräte ausgehen, wenn aber einer krank wird, kann er nicht an Land gebracht werden. Wir sind dann sozusagen Gefangene.

Unit 4   Die Interpretation eines Gedichts oder einer Kurzgeschichte

Viele Gedichte oder Prosatexte kann man ohne größere Schwierigkeiten lesen und verstehen. Sie gefallen einem auch, ohne daß man irgendeine besondere Hilfe braucht oder ein bestimmtes Fachwissen haben muß. Es gibt allerdings auch Gedichte oder erzählende Texte, die man selbst nach mehrmaligem Lesen nicht ganz versteht. Um solchen Kunstwerken ein Höchstmaß an Genuß abgewinnen zu können, muß man bestimmte Methoden der Interpretation erlernen.

Wenn man ein Gedicht interpretiert, sollte man auf folgende Punkte eingehen: Was sind Gegenstand und Thema des Gedichts? Welchen Schauplatz hat der Autor gewählt? Schafft das Gedicht eine besondere Atmosphäre? Wie ist der Charakter des Gedichts? Ist er ernst, heiter, förmlich, zwanglos, ironisch? Welche Bilder und Methaphern verwendet der Autor? Welche Rolle spielen Reimschema, Versmaß und Rhythmus eines Gedichts?

Der deutsche Leser eines englischen Gedichts sieht sich einem speziellen Problem gegenüber. Da Gedichte in einer Fremdsprache meist schwieriger zu verstehen sind als in der Muttersprache, muß der Leser besonders den Wortschatz beachten. Bestimmte Wörter können neben ihrer Grundbedeutung auch zusätzliche Bedeutungen haben, die besonders wichtig sind. Dichter verwenden solche Wörter häufig, in der Annahme, daß sie für die Leser unterschiedliche Beiklänge haben.

Auch wenn man ein Gedicht mehrere Male liest und die Methoden der Interpretation angewandt hat, bleiben oft noch Fragen offen, die jeder einzelne dann für sich beantworten muß. Man behauptet, daß ein Gedicht nicht durch den Dichter allein, sondern auch durch den Leser geschaffen werde.

Bei der Interpretation einer Kurzgeschichte sollte folgendes beachtet werden: Anfang, Mittelteil und Ende einer Kurzgeschichte haben verschiedene Funktionen. Der erste Teil enthält die Exposition, in der das Thema und die handelnden

Personen vorgestellt werden. Im Verlaufe der Geschichte erzeugt der Autor Spannung, die zumeist aus einem Konflikt entsteht, der in einem Höhepunkt gipfelt. Im Schlußteil wird dieser Konflikt dann einer Lösung zugeführt, deren Ausgang überraschend sein kann. Bei einer Kurzgeschichte mit ungewissem Ausgang sind die Leser aufgefordert, sich selbst ein mögliches Ende auszudenken. Eine oft verwendete Technik ist die Rückblende, in der Ereignisse beschrieben werden, die vor Beginn der eigentlichen Geschichte abliefen.